ACCLAIM FOR *THE GRIND*

"Sleepless pitchers, hopeful nomads, suitcase spouses. These are just some of the very real characters drawn with exquisite, page-turning insight by Barry Svrluga. *The Grind* enters the pantheon of must-read books about baseball."

—Sally Jenkins, *The Washington Post*

"*The Grind* . . . looks at the toll that the every-day-for-six-months-with-no-days-off pace takes on all sorts of people associated with the game and the oft-unseen sacrifices the sport requires."
—*The Wall Street Journal*

"If every era gets the baseball books it deserves, *The Grind* is definitely one for ours. Svrluga reveals a culture of nonstop stress: a relentless rhythm of scouting odysseys, training routines, travel monotony, injuries—all before anyone gets out on the field. No wonder these guys are obsessive. But they must also be undaunted. In our distracted, data-saturated age, grittier models of excelling would be hard to find."
—*The Atlantic*

"A little treasure."
—*Huffington Post*

"Whether baseball bores you or thrills you, *The Grind* offers a glimpse into what it feels like to be a part of a rarefied world punctuated as much by failure and frustration as glitz and glamour." —*Washington City Paper*

"Each subject offers a view into little-seen aspects of the baseball life and provides curious fans with new insight into the elements required to make an MLB game happen. *Verdict*: A quick and enjoyable read for any baseball lover, not just Nationals fans." —*Library Journal*

"It's no grind whatsoever to read Svrluga's flowing prose. An illuminating and entertaining must-read for the baseball obsessed." —*Kirkus Reviews*

"Baseball generates a rich sediment of numbers, but the one most difficult for fans to appreciate isn't about an exotic achievement—Ted Williams's .406 or Joe DiMaggio's 56-game hitting streak. Rather, it is 162, the number of games in a season. Readers of Barry Svrluga's splendid book will henceforth watch the game with deepened understanding, and the players with increased admiration." —George F. Will

"In *The Grind*, Barry Svrluga helps fans understand everything that happens outside the nightly three-hour window of the game—how we prepare, who helps us prepare, and what goes into a Major League season. Everyone in the clubhouse knows these stories. Few outside of it do."

—Ryan Zimmerman, Washington Nationals infielder

"Baseball's daily grind is the game's winnowing test of character. . . . In *The Grind*, Barry Svrluga captures this rich side of the sport with more color, detail, and insight than anyone before him. Svrluga's writing and reporting makes the game's toughest tasks a smooth pleasure for readers."

—Thomas Boswell, author of *Why Time Begins on Opening Day* and *How Life Imitates the World Series*

THE
GRIND

THE GRIND

Inside Baseball's Endless Season

o

BARRY SVRLUGA

BLUE RIDER PRESS

New York

blue
rider
press

An imprint of Penguin Random House LLC
375 Hudson Street
New York, New York 10014

The Library of Congress has catalogued the hardcover edition as follows:

Svrluga, Barry.
The grind : inside baseball's endless season / Barry Svrluga.
p.   cm
Includes bibliographical references and index.
ISBN 978-0-399-17628-9 (hardback)
1. Baseball—United States.   2. Baseball—Psychological aspects.
3. Baseball—Social aspects.   I. Title.
GV863.A1S945   2015   2015016056
796.357—dc23

Blue Rider Press hardcover edition: July 2015
Blue Rider Press paperback edition: March 2016
Blue Rider Press paperback ISBN: 978-0-399-57595-2

9780399575952

Printed in the United States of America
1   3   5   7   9   10   8   6   4   2

Original hardcover book design by Amanda Dewey

For Mom

CONTENTS

°

THE
GRIND

Introduction

In 1876, when the National League was founded, all of eight teams competed for a championship. The Philadelphia Athletics and the Boston Red Stockings staged the first game in league history on April 22, with the rest of the franchises starting their seasons over the ensuing days, beginning what was designed as a 70-game schedule that lasted until late September, five months to determine a title. The Chicago White Stockings easily made history, winning 52 of the 66 games they could complete, beating the Hartford Dark Blues by six games in the standings.

The White Stockings played those 66 games over 156 days, the schedule meandering through the heat of the summer to the edge of fall. With the league spread from Boston to St. Louis, from Louisville to New York, teams had to allow time for train travel. Still, even when in one place, the White Stockings never played on three consecutive days. They more frequently had back-to-back days off than back-to-back days with games. It was the kind of schedule that allowed right-hander Al Spalding to pitch in 61 games, starting 60, completing 53—all with a little rest in between.

Such a rhythm, if that's what it was, would be unrecognizable in today's major leagues. When I arrived at spring training in 2005 for my first season as a baseball beat writer for *The Washington Post*, I had only a fan's sense of the ebbs and flows of a season, and I understood only that each day brought new possibility. Standing in windswept Viera, Florida, the calendar to come was right there in front of me: pitchers and catchers reporting February 15, the first Grapefruit League game March 2, Opening Day not till April 4, consecutive days off not until July 11 and 12, 230 days until the last of 162 regular-season games would be played. It all stared back, sure to be full of unexpected celebrations and soon-to-be-identified story lines, but daunting all the same.

What I didn't understand then seems obvious now. A baseball season is a shared experience, an experience broken into tiny little sections—a pitch, an at-bat, a rally, an inning, a game, a series, a winning streak, a slump, a month, a summer. The fan sees all of those elements, shares in them, stringing together the nightly three-hour public performances. Watch the game enough, and its patterns become familiar and unmistakable, even as there's no way to know what will happen on the next pitch or the next night. As complicated as it can be, baseball leaves little mystery. A curveball is a curveball. Now, whether that curveball should have been thrown in a certain situation is part of the conversation, the common discourse that takes place on subways and sports talk radio each summer morning.

What I discovered, though, was that the shared experience is much deeper back up the tunnel from the dugout, into the clubhouse, onto the bus back to the hotel, and during the flight to the next city. Everyone in that community—players and managers and coaches, sure, but video analysts and media relations people and play-by-play guys and athletic trainers and clubhouse attendants and beat reporters, too—comes to understand it and deal with it, even thrive on it, individually. No one outside this bubble really knows it, comprehends it, so there's not much point discussing it beyond those parameters.

Inside, though, that day-to-day, game-to-game, city-to-city existence is chewed on and digested and discussed over and over again, even as it becomes an accepted way of life. A rain delay during the last night of a three-game series in, say, Cincinnati isn't just an opportunity for the broadcast teams to toss it back to the studio, for the television stations to fill the air with highlights from other games or sitcom reruns, until play resumes. Sure, players pass time with card games or movies or other frivolities. But the delay is a meaningful obstacle that must be overcome; it pushes back the team's flight, which pushes back its arrival in the next city, which pushes back the time when heads can hit pillows—four a.m.? five a.m.?—all with a game to play the next night.

Such tiny disruptions over the course of the season are, by now, cast against the modern backdrop, when a baseball player is a baseball player in January and in July, in winter as well as summer. Long after the White Stockings took that original National League championship, professional baseball remained an avocation as much as a career. Into the 1960s and even the '70s, players held offseason jobs not to fill the time but to feed their families. Yogi Berra worked at a Sears, Roebuck. Lou Brock became a florist. Players sold real estate and insurance, worked in mines and on ranches. Even before the White Stockings helped form the National League, Spalding started a sporting goods store in Chicago and eventually began manufacturing athletic equipment of all kinds, with a name that's still alive today.

Spring training was exactly that: training. Selling insurance or substitute teaching doesn't prepare a body for a baseball season, so players needed seven weeks in Florida or—back in the old days—Texas or Arkansas, California or Louisiana, all sorts of Southern destinations to get into shape.

The schedule, too, evolved from those sporadic games in 1876, expanding and contracting until settling at 154 games in 1904—three years after the identification of the American League as a major league—though there were occasional changes during wartime. When the American League expanded in 1961 and the National League in 1962, the 162-game season became the norm. Though further expansion has brought more tiers to the playoffs—pushing the World Series to the brink of November—the regular season hasn't wavered since. Somehow, it's perfect. Players know exactly what they must prepare for, what awaits them.

That first season the Nationals were in Washington—Major League Baseball relocated the Montreal Expos to end a thirty-three-year baseball drought in the nation's capital—their first baseman was a guy named Nick Johnson, a talented hitter whose career was interrupted time and again by injuries. Until you got to know him, Johnson was one of the all-time intentionally terrible interviews in baseball, drawing straight from the Kevin Costner character in *Bull Durham*, meaningless cliché followed only by an even worse meaningless cliché. At some point during the season, when I asked again about how he would approach a slump or a hot streak or something, Johnson shrugged. "Just keep grindin'," he said.

I thought about it then, and realized he had said it in spring training, during the season's first month when he was hot, during the early weeks of July when he was out with an injury, and after he returned and started to sputter at the plate. "Keep grindin'." Clichés, it turns out, are clichés for a reason. Johnson meant what he was saying. Head down. Eyes forward. Don't worry about the games that have passed or how many are ahead. Don't think about the city you're in or the state of your swing. Keep grindin'. There was no other approach.

When the 2014 season began, I was back covering baseball for the *Post*, and Johnson's quote—variations of which I had heard time and again over the ensuing years—stayed with me. There had to be a way to explain or show the impact of that grind on an entire organization. Position players are different from pitchers. Starters are different from relievers. Executives are different from scouts. The majors are different from the minors. Husbands are different from wives. But they all experience it to some degree or another. My editors at the *Post* allowed me to take a crack at explaining that phenomenon, one that's just outside the parameters of those three-hour games each night.

This book is the result. This book, it would seem, is about the Washington Nationals. But the characters in it and those around them will invariably agree: It could be about any of the thirty major league teams. In baseball, these themes are universal.

Each major league team has a veteran trying to overcome an injury and get ready for yet another season. Each has a player with a young wife juggling a family with her husband's career. Each has a scout racking up miles and hotel nights while pursuing the next star player. Each has a starting pitcher figuring out how to prepare on the four days no one sees him perform. Each is watching a player who has tasted major league success but is back in the minors, struggling to return. Each has a support staff that makes the trains run on time, even if no one understands how. Each has a reliever who has coughed up a ninth-inning lead but must return the next night. And each has a general manager overseeing it all, stepping back for a global view but obsessing about the details.

The schedule, those 162 games, is what we see, the part that can be folded up and put into our wallets and kept as a reference point. But for all those involved, it really just represents the contours of the season. That baseball players don't live like accountants or zookeepers is apparent. What they go through to live that way is not. Each day at the ballpark, there is the potential for joy—a game-winning hit, a game-saving catch, a game-ending strikeout. The route to that joy is far less understood.

Who knows whether the Chicago White Stockings of 1876 endured such stresses, and how they dealt with them if they did? By now, nearly 140 years later, the grind of a major league season is universal, shared by all the players and all those around them. For so many, it is the defining aspect of the national pastime.

RYAN ZIMMERMAN

The Veteran

On another cloudy morning of an endless winter, Ryan Zimmerman left his newborn daughter with his wife, hopped into his Chevrolet Tahoe, opened the gate at the end of his long driveway in McLean, Virginia, and drove down the road to the house of Jayson Werth, his teammate with the Washington Nationals, all of five minutes away. It was January 15, 2014, a Wednesday. It could have been the Wednesday after Christmas. It could have been the Wednesday before Valentine's Day. It could, absolutely, have been Groundhog Day.

At Werth's house, John Philbin and Matt Eiden, the Nationals' two strength-and-conditioning coaches, met with the pair of veterans, another day in the life. "I tell Matty," Werth said, "I'll wake up when you ring the bell."

And with that, in Werth's home gym—an offseason amenity built with the baseball season in mind—the two coaches did what they did the day before, and the day before that, and what they would do in the days to come: They goaded Werth and Zimmerman into lifting massive amounts of weight to put massive amounts of muscle on their bodies, all with the stifling heat of August and the chill of October in mind.

Spring training was a month away, the season still more than ten weeks off. When the games begin, all that muscle will deteriorate, eroded by the pounding surf that is the baseball season, coming at them wave after wave after wave.

"All you can do is try to maintain," Zimmerman said, "and survive."

There is no other sport with an everydayness, a *drum-drum-drum* beat like baseball. The Nationals opened their 2014 season in New York on the last day of March, a Monday, then had Tuesday off, protection against a rainout. Over the ensuing 26 days, they played 25 games. Six times during the season, they faced stretches of at least a dozen days, each with a game. Their first and only back-to-back days off—a worker bee's regular weekend—came in July. All told: 162 games in 182 days.

All sorts of professions—accounting and advertising, fishing and farming—come replete with their own rhythms. In professional sports, baseball's is uniquely unyielding. It might not feel that way in March, when Opening Day serves as such a symbol for spring, for hope. But the players know, the coaches know, the scouts and the families and, heck, even the concessionaires—they all know what lies ahead. And they all refer to it the same way, with unmistakable reverence: the grind.

"I don't think people realize what goes into a baseball season," Zimmerman said.

Professional hockey and basketball seasons involve a hair more than half as many games. Banged-up? Make it through one night, and take it easy at the next day's practice. There are, at minimum, three off days in a week. Three off days in a week of a baseball season would involve a couple of rain-outs. Banged-up baseball players?

"People think we just stand around on the field," Zimmerman said. "We don't. No other sport plays every day. Even hockey and basketball, they play a lot of games, but every week you have at least two days off at some point. If they play four games in a week, that's a bad week.

"So for them, if you're hurting a little bit, you can make it through one game knowing that you have a day off. We have maybe four off days a month—maybe. You can't hide it. You can't hide."

When he said this on January 15, his 90-minute workout at Werth's was finished. The kitchen of Zimmerman's house was drenched in afternoon light, the clouds having moved away. During the repetition of the baseball year, it is as hidden as he gets, tucked away in the Virginia woods with his new family. Yet the grind always serves as the backdrop. He was twenty-nine, so far removed from the day when he was drafted, the day that summer of 2005 when he made the majors at twenty. As an adult, the pattern of the baseball season—and the year that is propped up around it—is all Zimmerman has ever known.

"I think the only way to learn is to go through it," he said.

When he answered the door that day, he cradled the lightest weight he would handle all month, little Mackenzie, a healthy 8 pounds 5 ounces when she was born the previous November. He handed her off to his wife of barely a year, Heather, a newcomer to the churn.

"At first I kind of wished he had more of a normal job, I guess," Heather Zimmerman said. "Baseball was such a completely different lifestyle than I'd ever been aware even existed."

Miley, the couple's English bulldog, wandered in. In less than a month, this entire family operation would uplift for Viera, Florida, for six and a half weeks of spring training. Zimmerman leaned over to scratch Miley.

"It'll all start again," he said. Excitement mixed with a small degree of dread. It'll all start again. When it does, there's no escape.

J ust after seven p.m. on March 10, Zimmerman emerged from the home dugout at Space Coast Stadium in Viera, for his second at-bat of a game that will never be remembered, even by those who played in it, the Nationals and Houston Astros. The sun was setting across Viera, the hodge-podge of strip malls and new-home developments where the Nationals set up shop each spring. Zimmerman, too, shows up here every year, taking the massive cuts in the on-deck circle that he took that night, trying to get loose for that particular irrelevant game, for that particular irrelevant at-bat.

"It's just spring training," Zimmerman said. "It's hard to get up and get excited for playing down here. It drags on towards the end."

This would seem to be the beginning, a time when each pitch is part of the important process of building to the season. Yet in and of itself, none is especially significant. "Guys hit .600 in spring training," Zimmerman said. "Guys hit .200. It doesn't matter."

Zimmerman didn't swing a bat before he arrived in Florida. But hitting is routine enough for him that, with 4,366 lazy onlookers around him, he got a fastball on the outside part of the plate and drilled it to right field, the opposite way, a double.

Part of the grind, though, is the work it took to get even to that point, to rinse clean the cobwebs from the previous season and begin anew, building again. When he was twenty-one or twenty-two, Zimmerman would take a couple of weeks to let the season go before he began working out again. "I'd get bored," he said. Now, headed into his ninth full season, he takes a month—at least. No bats. No balls. No weights.

"During the season, you don't really feel it," Zimmerman said. "But as soon as the season is over, that first week you're just kind of still in shock. And that second week is where you're like, 'Man, that was a long, long run.' So you have to give yourself time to recover before you start getting at it again."

But by the holidays, Zimmerman and Werth—the only Nationals who live near Washington year-round—are working with Philbin and Eiden five or six times a week. There is nothing subtle about this portion of the baseball year. In so many ways, it is downtime. Increasingly, though, it has become essential to bulk up.

"You have to get as big and as strong as you can," Werth said. "I think what people don't realize is once the season starts, you just lose weight all the way to the end. . . . The grind is going to wear you down weight-wise and strength-wise. So that's our goal: Work as hard and try to get as big and strong as possible."

By the previous August, for instance, Nationals first baseman Adam LaRoche had lost nearly fifteen pounds from spring training. Sapped of strength, he tried to put on weight during the season, a futile pursuit. Zimmerman said he had been able to maintain his own ideal weight, about 220 pounds, through each of the previous six seasons. But it is because of the strength he builds in the offseason, so much lifting that when he begins throwing, "it's literally like learning how to throw again because you're so stiff."

Philbin, known in the clubhouse as Coach, is there to guide, both during the season and after. A former Olympic bobsledder who spent eight years as a strength coach with the Washington Redskins football team, he knows the violence of the NFL and what football players endure to recover from it and then build—over six days—to another game. Yet there is nothing, Philbin said, like the baseball season.

"It's just a different animal," he said. "They're not obviously in a contact sport, but yet physically, mentally, psychologically, and spiritually they have to get up and be at their best on a daily basis. And that can take its toll over time, because you mentally have to be there, too. That's hard to sometimes overcome. But you've got to. There's no days off."

Which is why time is so carefully managed during spring training. After Zimmerman doubled against the Astros, LaRoche lofted a fly ball to left, and Zimmerman began jogging around third. With the inning over, he continued his amble to the dugout, then the clubhouse, then home—before the game was over, his night done. It is a privilege afforded veteran players in spring training, an acknowledgment of the preparation already put in and the labor still to come: Get your work in, and get out of here. Rare is the veteran position player who sees the ninth inning of a Grapefruit League game.

Two days later, two men staffed a makeshift breakfast

station at one end of the long, simple home clubhouse, and the Nationals lined up, Styrofoam plates in hand, before eight a.m. Omelets made to order, pancakes with berries. On the bulletin board at the other end of the room hung two lists: a group of Nationals headed to Kissimmee to play the Astros, another headed to Lake Buena Vista to play the Braves. The night before, Zimmerman's name had been typed onto the first sheet, a rare spring road trip for a veteran. That morning, it was covered by black marker, a workday transformed to an off day.

"You have to not be sore anymore," Zimmerman said later, with the clubhouse nearly empty, its inhabitants having lugged their bags to two awaiting buses, each with a journey of more than an hour ahead.

It was 9:15. By this point in his day, Zimmerman had already spent time with athletic trainers, going over the various aches and pains, and put in a weight-lifting session, shortened by Philbin's orders to twenty-five minutes once the preseason games began.

At that point, Zimmerman had twice had surgery on his left wrist, once had surgery on his abdomen, and once had surgery on his right shoulder. Nationals manager Matt Williams, in the first year in his position but a veteran of seventeen years as a player, is well aware of all those dynamics with veterans—injuries and ailments, the balance between proper preparation and essential rest.

"You ask a young player, you know you're not necessarily

going to get the truth," Williams said. "'How you feeling?' 'Great.' But the veteran guys seem to tell you."

The day before, Werth was due up for the third time in a game against St. Louis. "When you get on here," Williams asked him, "do you want to run the bases?" In preparing for what's ahead, there is no bit of minutia not worth discussing. "That stuff matters," Werth said.

With his treatment and workout over and the home clubhouse nearly empty, Zimmerman sat at his locker and fiddled with a new putter as so many of his teammates traveled across the state to play games. Even in March, even in Florida, veterans must have the push through July and August in mind, those moments after you're stranded on base, and you stand in the middle of the diamond waiting for a teammate to deliver your glove, and it's 92 degrees and your mind wanders, and then the next pitch is right there and you have to be locked in.

"You see it in guys," said veteran infielder Jamey Carroll, who was trying to make the Nationals at age forty. "Then you talk about it, and you feel it yourself. It's like saying 'red truck' and all of a sudden you see all the red trucks around. You wonder how young guys will do this year, their first long season at this level with the extra pressure, the media, the travel, the stuff that I think adds up. No matter what you do, no matter how you handle it, it's hard."

By ten a.m., Zimmerman walked out the back door to the clubhouse, done for one day. He had been in Florida more than three weeks. The season was still nearly three weeks away.

By that point in his career—1,137 games, 4,493 plate appearances, both more than anyone ever for the Nationals—there was little about the game that fazed Zimmerman, a fact that can come off as nonchalance. "He's a very regimented, type-A person," Heather Zimmerman said. "But he's very low-key about it. He's very quiet, and he just sort of has everything laid out in his mind as far as an agenda."

Yet so many nights the previous summer, when he made the drive down I-395 to the George Washington Parkway and on home after games, the agenda in his mind was jumbled. From the day he was selected with the fourth overall pick in the 2005 draft, Zimmerman could do one thing better than anything else: field his position. And here he was, unable to do it. Each time a grounder found its way into his glove, the ensuing throw—made with his surgically repaired right shoulder—became a hold-your-breath adventure.

In April, with two outs in the ninth inning and the Nats up by a run against Atlanta, Zimmerman fielded a grounder. A good throw ends the game. Zimmerman threw it away. The Braves won in ten. It began a stretch in which he made four errors in five games. Just twenty-two games into the year, he had seven errors.

"I've never felt uncomfortable on a baseball field," Zimmerman said. "It's embarrassing."

Here is the worst part of any season, when struggles—all endured publicly—make it feel stifling, inescapable. The previous June, Zimmerman's shoulder wasn't allowing him to drive the ball at the plate. "I was hitting third, and I was an out," he said. He was saved by a cortisone shot, and that's how he ground his way through the season: Live off the medicine until the medicine wears off, then get another shot.

Surgery was supposed to cure all that. It didn't, not immediately anyway. The grind wears on the body in untold ways. But that may not compare to what it does to the mind.

"The year before, I was working with the trainers just changing up everything [with his throwing motion] to try and basically just get through the season and get to the surgery," Zimmerman said. "That was awkward and obviously embarrassing to not be able to just blend in—in front of forty thousand people every day, when you're getting paid millions of dollars—and do what you're supposed to be able to do.

"Then I get through the surgery, and try to get myself to the point where I had a normal throwing motion, but to learn it again not in Florida on rehab but in New York on Saturday night, when we're ahead 2–1 and there's runners on second and third and someone hits me a ground ball to where if I throw it in the shitter we lose the game . . ."

He was sitting in his kitchen. He exhaled. "That's

mentally trying," he said. Heather Zimmerman noticed her husband, who barely talks baseball at home, growing a bit quieter about everything. Instead of going out to dinner with friends, they spent idle time on the couch.

"I don't think 'stressed' is part of Ryan's nature," said his agent, Brodie Van Wagenen of CAA Sports, to whom Zimmerman is close. "Ryan has had the good fortune that the game has always come very easy to him. The game is often played in slow motion for him. As a result, from an outside perspective, it looks like he's never stressed and is always in control.

"Not that Ryan's not the same player, but the game isn't always as easy as time goes on."

Such is the arc of a career. In other professions, it might be odd for someone in his twenties to make allowances for age. But even before the shoulder issues ate at him, even before a wife and child, Zimmerman had adjusted his lifestyle.

"From age twenty to twenty-five, you can do whatever you want and be fine," he said. "You can eat whatever you want. You can go out and have a few drinks on a Saturday night and grab dinner, and have a Sunday day game and be perfectly fine.

"But as you get older, you go to dinner, have one glass of wine, you go to bed. You have to learn your limits."

On those days that he couldn't throw, he felt physically limited. Mentally, he felt frazzled. Players can become consumed by such a situation. Managers must monitor them.

"The mental day off that managers give guys? There's some validity to that," Williams said. "But it doesn't necessarily work."

What works now, for Zimmerman, has long since been determined. Over the final two months of the 2013 season, his shoulder strengthened. In his final 21 games, he didn't make an error. So as the season wore on, his mind freed up, too.

"There's times when I doubted if I was ever going to be the same again, and that wears on you," Zimmerman said. "I think I have to go out and do it for this whole year before myself and other people really believe."

Another whole year sat at his feet. In so many ways, what was to come was unpredictable. But in so many others, it was exactly what he had lived before, one game bleeding into the next. No rest till October.

"Or November," he said.

CHELSEY DESMOND WITH SONS GRAYSON AND CRUZ

The Wife

The preparation for the baseball season, sprawling and yawning before them, began in 30-minute increments in a rented Florida apartment at bedtime during spring training. Chelsey Desmond took her two sons—Grayson, then approaching his third birthday, and Cruz, just fifteen months old—to bed in Viera, across the state from the hometown where she and her husband, Ian, grew up, where they live still. At seven p.m., Cruz hit the pillow, done till daytime. At around nine, Grayson followed. The next night, they shifted to seven-thirty and nine-thirty. The night after, eight and ten.

Any project involving toddlers requires adjustments, and occasionally it took a couple of nights for a change to take hold. But when it was time to head north to Washington for

the season, the transition was complete. The offseason schedule evolved into the baseball schedule, with tykes as third-
shifters, staying up past midnight, waking up at ten or
eleven a.m.

There are 81 games to attend at Nationals Park, and try
making Chelsey miss one, whether bronchitis or bad moods
get in the way. There are 81 more to watch on television,
when Daddy's on the road and the Mid-Atlantic Sports Network provides the lone link. Chelsey Desmond knows what
other young mothers might think, knows what grandmothers
think, knows what schoolteachers think. You keep your kids
up till *when*?

The explanation can come with a sigh, internal or out
loud. Yes. Yes we do. Think it through. With Ian's departure
for the ballpark each day around one or 1:30 p.m. and return
after 11:00 p.m., try keeping the kids on a schedule the rest of
the world would deem "normal." When would the kids see
their dad?

"This is about staying together as a family," Chelsey said.

"Baseball wife" would seem to be a glamorous job: hair
done up, shopping all day, makeup just right, nannies at the
ready, clapping for your millionaire man from the stands,
then hugging him before rolling home in the SUV, tinted
windows up. That it is not. It is, at its core, an odd existence.
Baseball wives are expected to wed at a certain time of year,
to give birth at a certain time of year, to pick up the toys and
the car and the dogs and the kids when Dad is sent to the

minors or traded midseason. They are full-time moms, part-time real estate agents, occasional fathers, all-hours dog walkers, logistical magicians.

Let's be clear: This is not a complaint. "Being in D.C., you see all the military people," Ian Desmond said. "They're not worried about their husband coming home from a road trip. They're worried about their husband coming home alive."

It is, though, a reality. There is no sport like baseball, in which the seven and a half months from the start of spring training to the final regular-season game contains just one equivalent of a weekend, the all-star break. So there's no marriage like a baseball marriage, in which the players are in charge of their careers, and the wives are in charge of everything else.

"For half the year, you're like a single mom," Ian Desmond said. "And you're a single mom in a city where you have no support. It's not like you're at home and you've got your family and friends that can keep eyes on kids. It's completely different."

Or, as Chelsey Desmond said, "People think it's all roses and butterflies."

There are those, and she knows it. She said this with her twenty-seven-year-old legs curled up underneath her in a leather chair in the living room of their rented house on a leafy street in Arlington, Virginia. On the bare floor of the adjacent dining room, there was no table, only a stroller and a scooter so Grayson and Cruz and Bailey, the family's affectionate pit bull, had plenty of space to roam. The clock on the wall stood stuck at 8:50.

Glamour? Chelsey's uniform for the morning—for just about *every* morning—was sneakers, Lululemon sweats, headband in hair, coffee in hand. The Disney Channel played quietly in the background, but Grayson picked up a plastic baseball bat instead. Ian sat slumped in a facing couch, both a crippling error and a monstrous home run twelve hours behind him. Another game stared him, and the family, straight in the face.

"Go to Daddy's game?" Grayson said. "Go to Daddy's game?"

"Not now," Chelsey Desmond said. "Not yet."

"Where's Cruz?" Ian asked. Now seventeen months old, Cruz had wandered off, behind the island in the kitchen.

On the agenda for this Tuesday: nothing. It is essential. "This is the time we get with Ian," Chelsey said. "Without this time, what would we have?"

In any profession, there are experiences that only colleagues can truly understand. Accountants have accountant complaints, and oh what the specter of April 15 must feel like. Ditch diggers have ditch digger complaints, and here comes the heat of summer. Hedge fund managers? Don't get them going, because it's all kinds of stress to make millions of dollars.

Baseball wives, then, are their own club. "I always joke that when you get traded they kind of throw you into the family room and say, 'Pick a friend,'" said Lory Ankiel, wife of former Nationals outfielder Rick. "And you think about it. What if I would not be friends with any of these girls? Who would understand?"

Very few people. Wives of NFL players might relocate to another city to follow their husbands' careers, might even raise their families there. But football players essentially have day jobs. Even late film study gets them home in time for dinner, in time for bedtime stories. Road trips last one night, and there are ten all year—counting preseason. There is hardly any midseason movement.

Contrast it all to baseball, in which six games a week are at night, in which swapping players is commonplace. So trade-deadline deals are every baseball family's worst fear. "A nightmare," Chelsey Desmond said, and she only has heard tell. In 2013, outfielder Scott Hairston was at a movie in Chicago with his wife, Jill, and their two sons. All cell phones were off, and when the family emerged, text messages and voice mails awaited; Scott had been traded from the Cubs to the Nationals. They wanted him on a flight that night.

"He had to pack something," Jill Hairston said. He did,

and left the next morning. She packed up the house and the kids.

In 2010, Lory Ankiel was pregnant with her first child when Rick was dealt from Kansas City to Atlanta. He left. She stayed. She packed up the clothes, the pictures, the Rottweiler, and the Siberian husky, and drove home to Jupiter, Florida, before turning around and heading to Atlanta to find a new place and start a new life. Temporarily.

There has to be a better way, she thought. So she started a Web site, ourbaseballlife.com, which offers resources in every major league city—vets, pediatricians, real estate agents, approved babysitters, and so on. The service could replace the informal word of mouth that has kept baseball families socially afloat for generations.

"I would have no clue about where to send him to school," Chelsey Desmond said, looking at Grayson. But why look in Washington now, when Grayson isn't even a kindergartner and Ian could be a free agent after the 2015 season? For now, it's enough to find an Arlington program in which Grayson can play soccer on Friday mornings.

"It's really easy to come to the field and let him be friends with the kids here," Ian Desmond said. "But you have to kind of put them in other social environments, where it's not only baseball players' kids. There are other kids who have no idea about baseball, who want to play something else or talk about something else. He should know them, too. You have to make an effort to do it."

These are, at a lot of levels, joint careers in which the labor might be divided but the stress is shared. Sitting in the stands, even now, Ian's younger brother Chris, who lived with the Desmonds during the 2014 season, will turn to his sister-in-law as her jaw clenches and say, "It's not the World Series, you know." When the Nationals made it to the postseason in 2012, Chelsey found out something else. "You *do not* want to sit by me in the playoffs."

"When he goes through struggles, you feel it," she said. "I probably let it affect me too much."

The previous night, with the Nationals holding a 1–0, eighth-inning lead over the Los Angeles Angels, Ian Desmond failed to make a play he normally would make, an error that opened the gate for the Angels, who scored four times in the frame. In the ninth, Desmond crushed a solo homer to center, but the Nationals lost.

"I don't care about the homer," Ian Desmond said the next day, in his living room.

"I knew not to say anything about it," Chelsey Desmond said, sitting in that chair across the living room from her husband. "Not even, 'Nice job.'"

"She gets I'm still gonna be upset," Ian said. "The hardest part is getting over it now. 'Shake it off.' People say that. But it still affects you. Obviously I don't want it to affect my family. But how can I just fake it?"

"Yes, I understand," Chelsey said. "But I still sometimes feel like, 'Don't you want to talk about it?'"

She knows, though. She knows because she was an athlete herself, and the yearning for competition never completely leaves that kind of person. She knows, too, because she knows him. All baseball wives share, to some extent, the excitement and tension of their husbands' careers. Chelsey Desmond has shared in her husband's entire life.

"To me, he wasn't Ian Desmond, baseball player," she said. "He was Ian Desmond from fifth grade."

It was in the lunchroom at Ashton Elementary School in Sarasota, Florida. Ian Desmond walked in wearing the T-shirt from a baseball tournament in which he had participated, the strut of a ten-year-old athlete. And like in any good love story, even good love stories that begin before puberty, little Chelsey Edwards whipped her head around and said, "*Who's that?*" She looked at the names of the team members listed on the back of the shirt, at all those she recognized. "It's not him. It's not *him*."

So it began. They "dated" in fifth grade, then again in middle school—that is, until Ian talked Chelsey into a trade with another boy. Kid stuff. But what Ian likes now was there then. He can still tell Chelsey's mother about the sundress Chelsey wore in her fifth-grade class picture, because she never wore a dress in her life. "That's part of the reason I married her," he said. She was a tomboy, soccer and softball and volleyball, good enough to score more goals than anyone in the history of Riverview High, good enough to earn a scholarship to Lynn University down in South Florida.

Chelsey Edwards was a Sarasota homebody, though, enough that when it came time to go to college, she freaked out. She decided to stay home, enrolled in community college, and hoped to become a dental hygienist.

Ian had his own scholarship, his to the University of South Florida, but when the Montreal Expos took him in the third round of the 2004 draft, he signed. In October 2005, after his first full season of pro ball, he officially asked Chelsey to be his girlfriend.

His life was off, a complete dedication to baseball with no guarantee it would pay off. Her life, in a way, began anew. In 2006, when he was playing at Class A Potomac, he stayed with a local family and would talk with Chelsey for hours by phone sitting in his car out front, so as not to disturb his hosts. The first time she came to visit, her luggage got lost, Ian's car broke down, and they had to bum a ride over to Potomac Mills Mall to buy some sweats and T-shirts so she could get through the trip.

By then, Chelsey was working in a dentist's office and had demands on her time. "I didn't care if they fired me," she said. She would follow the team bus, learning the back roads of the minors, from Woodbridge, Virginia, to Myrtle Beach, South Carolina, and back again, only to have to pay for her own hotel room in whatever dump the team stayed at. Neither made much money. They might not see each other for a month or more. There were external pressures, too.

"When you're dating a baseball player, all anyone wants to tell you is, 'He's cheating on you,'" Chelsey said.

This is the hushed-tones subculture of baseball, that of infidelity. Chelsey said she took solace in the fact that she had known Ian for so long, through so much. He didn't go out much, and doesn't to this day. They are, by their own telling, both introverts.

"He was the best boyfriend ever," Chelsey said. "He was aware of my feelings. I didn't ever have to worry."

Yet laying the foundation for a baseball life meant stress anyway. During one surprise visit from Chelsey and his family, on the road in New Hampshire, Ian got a message to meet Harrisburg manager John Stearns in the hotel lobby. Stearns delivered the news: He was demoted from Class AA to Class A. Chelsey joined Ian's mother in driving him to the airport the next morning. Both women sobbed.

"Is this even worth it?" Chelsey said she and Ian would ask each other. "Why are we torturing ourselves?"

The torture eventually subsided. It was, it turned out, worth it. In the fall of 2008, the Nationals sent Ian to the Arizona Fall League, where only elite prospects go. The couple got engaged, and the next day, the Nationals added Ian to the forty-man roster—another major step, an indication that security and stability might actually exist in this game. It meant, essentially, that the Nationals valued him and saw him as part of the future. The next spring, before he departed for the season, he left a note for his mother, something he did every year. This time it read: "This is going to be the year when I'm going to make it to the big leagues."

In September, he was called up. And there was Chelsey, watching his first major league appearance—in which he hit both a homer and a double back in Washington—on television with her family in Sarasota, then driving through the night to meet her fiancé at the team hotel in Miami. She got out of her Honda Accord to find—what's this?—a valet. Her hair was on top of her head. She wore sweats and a T-shirt. Ian Desmond had just one game in the majors, and even he knew: That's not how major league girlfriends dress.

"Welcome to the big leagues," Chelsey said. "I was so out of my element."

The next night, with Chelsey in the stands, Ian went 4 for 4.

On a Monday night in May, when the skies opened up at Nationals Park, the games continued under the concourses, just outside the home clubhouse. Grayson and Cruz Desmond jitterbugged about, each dressed in a little Nationals jersey with little Nationals pants, each wearing number 20 with "Desmond" stitched across the back. Grayson tugged a plastic bat. Cruz tossed a tiny rubber baseball.

"We're staying," Chelsey Desmond said, maybe midway through what became a rain delay of more than three hours, sinking into a couch. "I could try to get them to leave, but Grayson wouldn't have it."

She sat across from Jen LaRoche, wife of first baseman Adam and mother of two, on another couch. Jill Hairston, wife of outfielder Scott and mother of two more, leaned back in a chair. They were the only Nationals wives left during the deluge, and the only three who had their kids in Washington before the end of the school year. The televisions on the walls carried the Cardinals and Braves, and each woman knew exactly what was at stake: If Atlanta lost for the seventh straight time and the Nationals beat the Dodgers when the rain ended, their husbands would be in first place. A Brave smacked a home run. Three adult women yelled, "No. Nooooooooo!"

Grayson Desmond wandered over to the refrigerator. "I want a Popsicle," he said, tugging at the door. "Have some fruit, Grayson," said his mom.

During the season, the family room is a baseball wife's refuge. Players pay for their families' tickets to games, yet some families rarely use the seats. The family room is the Nationals' hub, with two sitters on hand, toys in a back room, an open play area to throw around a ball outside the door—a makeshift yard. Handprints from an art project are smeared across one wall. This offseason, the walls were repainted a bright red and white, the Nationals' colors.

Not every team affords families such a space.

"I feel like I want to scream at some GMs: 'Do you have any clue?'" Lory Ankiel said. "I know there's an old-school way of thinking, that the men just do the work. But to me it's logical. You can relieve so much stress on your player if you relieve the stress on his wife."

Sitting around during that rain delay, with their husbands in the clubhouse across the hall, there was little apparent stress among the wives. The LaRoches' two kids, twelve-year-old Drake and ten-year-old Montana, are fixtures at the ballpark. "She makes it look so easy," Chelsey Desmond said of Jen LaRoche. The Hairstons, with sons now eight and six, are pros, too. Last year, Jill Hairston hit thirteen cities with her family, sending postcards to the classrooms back home as something of a follow-the-Hairstons school project.

Chelsey Desmond is still, by her own admission, figuring it all out, with more figuring to come. Her husband signed a two-year, $17.5 million contract that would provide more money than either had ever dreamed of—but he hadn't signed on long-term with the Nationals. Who knows? Moves could be afoot. Chelsey was also pregnant with the couple's third child. The due date: October 18, smack in the middle of the postseason. When Grayson was born, Ian flew to Washington with the team from Pittsburgh, then hopped a flight to Tampa early the next morning, racing to Sarasota in time to witness the birth of their firstborn. In the spring of

2014, though, the Desmonds had to prepare for the potential confluence of playoffs and labor.

"I won't even tell him if I go into labor," Chelsey Desmond said.

It is a baseball life. "I get to support my husband living his dream," she said. "Not everyone can say that. There will never be any negative to that."

It was after ten p.m. in the family room. The tarp was still on. The Cardinals hung on to beat the Braves. And when the eighteenth home game of the Nationals' season ended after one a.m., Chelsey Desmond took her family home. Cruz stayed up much of the night, yet it didn't matter. On Tuesday, another game awaited the Desmonds, the entire Desmond family.

KRIS KLINE

The Scout

The eastbound lanes of Interstate 20 were dominated by 18-wheelers after dark, and Kris Kline deftly feathered his rented Nissan Altima among them as nine p.m. flew by and ten p.m. approached, the sun long since set behind him. Three baseball games cluttered his rearview mirror, too, back in the Birmingham suburb of Hoover, Alabama, and as he crossed the Georgia state line, another hotel room, another predawn shower, another flight, and three more baseball games the next day awaited him. He was tired.

Kline's last trip home to the Phoenix suburbs had been . . . well, wait. When was that? "Couple weeks ago, I guess," he said. Unimportant, really. What mattered was the first baseman from Kentucky and the four at-bats Kline just saw. What mattered was the bed at the Atlanta Airport Marriott Gateway, a 5:15 a.m. alarm, a tram through the darkness to the terminal, and Delta 1543 to Greensboro, North Carolina. What mattered was the next day, the next ballpark, the right-hander from the University of Maryland and the reliever from the University of Virginia who waited there.

"The hardest part of this job is getting to the job," Kline said. "Once I'm at the ballpark, I'm kind of at peace."

Kline wore jeans, a Columbia PFG fishing shirt, an Under Armour baseball hat, reading glasses when he made notes, wraparound shades when he didn't. "Total slob," he said. Only his title is fancy: Washington Nationals Assistant General Manager and Vice President of Scouting Operations.

Cross all that out. He's a scout. During that time, in late May, there are no more important people in the Nationals organization—not ace pitcher Stephen Strasburg, not young stud outfielder Bryce Harper—than Kline and the team of seventeen full-time scouts, plus two part-timers, he oversees. The big league Nationals played that night in Pittsburgh, earning their millions. Baseball's amateur draft was two weeks off, so Kline drove east into the night, searching for more players.

During the season, major leaguers live baseball day-to-day, and each evening can bring with it exhilaration—a rally-killing strikeout, a walk-off hit, a victory, with everyone lining up to high-five and celebrate in front of thirty or forty thousand in the stands and hundreds of thousands more on their couches.

Scouts live that same grind in the shadows. The exhilaration is subtle and would scarcely be recognized as such by people outside their insular world. No one knows about all the trips to Weather.com, wondering if a high schooler's game is going to be rained out, if itineraries must be juggled midstream to make sure no day passes without seeing a game. No one knows about arriving at a college campus on a Friday with the singular goal of seeing the closer, then waiting all weekend before the manager finally decides to use him on Sunday. No one knows about the time Kline was with the Arizona Diamondbacks on a one-year contract, fighting for his job. He rented a hotel room in Texas for a month, drove to see players all over the state, then headed up Interstate 55 toward the Arkansas-Tennessee border.

There, a tractor-trailer truck rear-ended his Crown Victoria, the company car. He dusted himself off, tied the trunk shut with a shoelace, and lugged it to a shop. He rented another car and kept driving. Days later, the phone rang. It was his boss, Mike Rizzo, then the scouting director in Arizona, now the Nationals' general manager.

"Where are you?" Rizzo asked.

"Kent, Ohio," Kline said.

"What the hell are you doing in Kent, Ohio?" Rizzo said.

Well, there was this right-hander, you see, kid named

Dirk Hayhurst, who played for Kent State. And he has a teammate, too, probably should see him.

"Get your ass home right now," Rizzo ordered.

Kline hardly realized it, but he'd been gone for almost two months. Most scouts have a story like that. Kline has 1.2 million Marriott points. He once called Southwest Airlines wondering whether he had enough miles to buy his daughter a round-trip ticket for a visit; the nice woman on the other end of the phone told him he had enough miles for thirty-five round-trips. The profession does not marry ideally with self-preservation, nor does it marry ideally with, well, marriage.

"I missed a lot," Kline said, thinking of his twenty-four-year-old son and twenty-one-year-old daughter. "A lot."

And yet: "People spend their whole life trying to find the one thing you love doing. I've found it. I don't need to do that."

He was fifty-two and long divorced, and that January he quit chewing tobacco for the first time in thirty years. Almost immediately, he added twenty pounds to his 6-foot-4 frame. "I'm a little husky," he said, drawing out the adjective, making sure it was a self-deprecating assessment. He can flip through his iPhone to show a grandfatherly allotment of photos of his grandson, nearly three, smiling broadly at each one. His next trip home would come that Saturday morning, to be there for his daughter's birthday.

But before then, there were still sixty miles of interstate to cover in darkness, still another flight to catch. Other scouts from other clubs would see the right-hander from Maryland, the reliever from Virginia. Kline had to get there, too.

Earlier that day, there wasn't a cloud in the high sky above Hoover Metropolitan Stadium, and the seats behind home plate at the Southeastern Conference baseball tournament filled with scouts wearing broad-brimmed fishing hats, scouts with wet towels draped over their necks, scouts with white zinc smeared on their faces, maybe sixty guys in all. "I'm smokin'," Kline said. Sweat ran down his neck.

Kline got to the ballpark at 8:30 a.m., an hour before the day's first pitch. When Kentucky and Florida took the field late in the afternoon, he left Mark Baca, another of the Nationals' scouts, in the seats behind the plate. Kline needed to get another look at Kentucky's designated hitter that day, a power-hitting junior named A. J. Reed who normally played first base. Because Reed hits left-handed, Kline took a seat along the left-field line, a better vantage point from which to see his swing.

"I hope A.J. strikes out four times," Kline said. "I really do."

He didn't want other scouts to learn what he already knew. "He will hit," he said, "and he will hit for power." But the general managers from the Marlins and the Diamond-backs were each down the left-field line as well, not by coin-cidence, and they were joined by scouts from the Yankees, the Tigers, on and on. Kline already knew what he thought of "the player"—and that's how scouts talk, referring to these sons and nephews and boyfriends in the most generic ways. Late one night when he was home in Arizona, he flipped on one of Reed's games he had recorded on his DVR. Reed jacked a massive homer clear over the batter's eye in center field at Tennessee.

"I turned it off," Kline said. "That was enough."

So these trips, late in the process of evaluating players for the draft, are about fine-tuning, reinforcing what scouts already thought or raising doubts where none existed before. Kline usually feels comfortable that he knows a hitter if he sees eight at-bats. In the first inning, Reed foul-tipped a 2-2 pitch into the glove, a strikeout on a 93-mph fastball. Kline didn't flinch. Add it to the file.

"People will think this is silly, but as a player, you get in the season and get in a groove, and the game slows down," he said. "That happens to me. The first week in a hotel, and you're back at it. You're watching a player, and you get into that rhythm. You're like, 'I know that guy. I like that guy.' You *know*."

He looked around Hoover Met, dotted with scouts.

"We're all locked in," he said. "We all know who we want. We all know who we like."

It's because the process began not that week or that month or even that year. Baca had scouted Reed in high school, three years earlier. "A kid I've always been drawn to," he said. Scouts begin building their own books on the next year's draft class the summer before, when high school kids appear in massive "showcases" and college kids spend time in elite wood-bat leagues. In February, they hit the road, five or six or seven games in a week, Miami one day, Oklahoma City the next.

The college conference tournaments in late May are smorgasbords, so many players in just one place. It's why Kline and Baca got back to their hotel at midnight on a Tuesday after a full day of games and were on site for batting practice prior to Vanderbilt and LSU at 9:30 a.m. Wednesday, then Arkansas and Ole Miss just after noon, then Kentucky and Florida, with Mississippi State and South Carolina still to come, under the lights.

"You have to love it," Baca said. "You have to have a passion for it."

Baca and Kline have worked together since 2001, when Rizzo was the scouting director in Arizona and hired Baca away from the Montreal Expos. Baca's title is "National Supervisor," but he is what's known in the industry as a "cross-checker"—a scout who could go anywhere at any time, following the recommendations of the area scouts of whom he needs to see. He filters information to Kline, and by this point in their lives, they're "like brothers," Kline said, or even an old married couple, bickering not about who should take out the trash but about whether a pitcher's off-speed stuff will play in the majors. They talk four or six or eight times a day by phone.

"He'll say, 'Why are you in such a bad mood today?'" Kline said. "And I'll just say, 'It's not you. It's me.'"

So they argue. Baca and Kline are unafraid to share their opinions on players with each other, with the Nationals' other cross-checkers—Jeff Zona, Fred Costello, and Jimmy Gonzales—and with Rizzo. That's what they're paid to do.

"The player will tell you what he is," Kline said. "They always do."

When Reed stepped into the box for his second at-bat, Kline needed to complete his opinion of him. What did it mean that he swung through a high fastball for his second straight strikeout? What did it mean in the fifth, when Reed drove the first pitch he saw high off the wall in right-center, a double that would have been a homer in almost any other park?

By the time of Reed's fourth at-bat, the lights had flickered on at Hoover Met. "I'm fading," Kline said. But he had to see Reed one more time, this against Florida lefty Kirby Snead. And here came one more bit of confusing information, Snead with a pair of back-to-back changeups, Reed with a pair of flailing swings, his third strikeout in four at-bats.

"I have to figure that out," Kline said as he got up. Where does that one game fit into the whole picture of the kid? How does he "profile," as scouts say? When Baca got to his computer the next day, he scrambled to look up Reed's splits against left-handers in case he had a glaring weakness the Nationals had overlooked.

After Kentucky beat Florida, only one player remained for Kline and Baca to see, a reliever from Mississippi State. Kline knew, though, what awaited: the drive across I-20 to Atlanta, the flight to Greensboro in the morning. He knew, too, there was no guarantee the kid would even pitch. "I'm just trying to be realistic," he said. This, though, ran counter to every instinct he had. See more. Dig deeper.

"If I'm not at a game, I feel like I'm always going to miss something," he said. "I hate that feeling. *I hate it.*"

Yet by 7:40 p.m., he walked through the stadium parking lot and pressed the fob on the keys to his rental car, hoping the Altima would beep and let him know where he parked it eleven hours earlier. The hotel was 160 miles away, the draft in two weeks. His back was sore. His legs ached.

"Hit a wall," he said. He fired up the car and drove into the Alabama night.

The next morning, when Kline settled into a seat at Gate A30, coffee and muffin in hand, he watched the line form to board: a scout for the Blue Jays, the Diamondbacks' scouting director, another scout with the Rays. They know one another, all these guys, some for most of their lives, and it can be a catty community, filled with inside jokes and shared information, old women in a quilting circle.

"I won't talk about players," Kline said. "But if someone else wants to talk about them, I'll definitely listen."

He has, though, talked the business to death. In 1983, he was an infielder in the Angels' chain, trying to make it in pro ball. His roommate that summer in Peoria, Illinois, was an infielder from Chicago named Mike Rizzo. Neither had a major league future. Rizzo hit .247 over three minor league seasons, Kline .262 over four. Yet they'd finish their own game, then head to a bar in hopes of finding one on television. They talked about teammates, about opponents.

"Neither of us really had any other interests," Rizzo said. "I often ask him, 'What would you do if you weren't in baseball?' He has no answer for it. I have no answer for it."

So they set off as baseball nomads, Kline as a scout for the Angels, Rizzo for the White Sox. Each served initially as an "area scout," responsible for a specific geographic region. That job is filled with tedium: calling coaches for pitching schedules, driving countless miles to high school games, talking with families and friends to learn players' histories, their other interests, their favorite ice cream flavors. Rizzo made $11,000 his first season, the first of twelve in which he served as an area scout. Now those scouts make around $30,000. Rizzo calls it the most important job in the scouting chain.

"It's a lot like the territorial salesman, where you have an area that you control," Rizzo said. "You run it. You need to know every in and out of that area—every high school coach, every college coach, every player, and every player's family. You have to be a self-starting type of guy, and you have to be willing to spend a lot of time alone. And then you pack your car up for about a month at a time, and you just drive."

The area scouts, in industry lingo, raise a flag to get the cross-checkers in to see players, a process that takes all spring. But when Kline pulled his rental car into the parking lot outside NewBridge Bank Park in Greensboro for the Atlantic Coast Conference tournament, he thought he knew whom he wanted to see: Maryland right-hander Jake Stinnett and Virginia closer Nick Howard, whose teams would face each other in the day's first game.

Kline met Gonzales in the concourse behind home plate. He bought a 32-ounce soda. "I gotta go home so I can get some new clothes," Gonzales said, and they went over notes from the games Gonzales had seen the day before. Crowds of grade schoolers who had been given free tickets filed into the seats as "Let It Go" from the Disney movie *Frozen* blared over the public address system at an unspeakably loud level, leading to shrieks from the children, completely obscuring the impending game and the scouts' task.

Yet when Stinnett took the mound, baseball began, and a couple of dozen radar guns rose in the seats behind the plate. Kline doesn't carry one, because he can always find someone to help him out. He poached Stinnett's first fastball off a scout who sat two rows in front of the concourse, where Kline chose to stand: 94 mph.

He pulled out a small notebook from his pocket. Since he began his travels in February, he had written reports on more than 150 players, all of whom he believed could play in the majors. Going back generations, scouts have graded on a 20-to-80 scale, with 50 being average for a major leaguer. Pitchers will be graded on their delivery and on their specific pitches, with notes about whether they throw easily or with maximum effort. (The former is preferable.) Hitters are graded on the five basic tools: hitting for average, hitting for power, defense, arm, and speed.

Kline never rates anyone as an 80, unless it's on pure speed, like former Nationals minor leaguer Billy Burns, who was traded to Oakland. He rarely hands out a 70, with the arm of current Nationals infielder Danny Espinosa an exception.

"If I put a 60 on a tool, I'm saying he's going to be above average," Kline said. "If he exceeds those expectations, great."

In the seventh inning, Maryland held a lead over Virginia, and the scouts' chances of seeing Howard were dwindling. Kline peeked at the radar gun a couple of rows in front of him after another Stinnett fastball: down to 89. He was tiring. Two innings later, Maryland's closer struck out a Virginia hitter for the final out of a 7–6 victory. Howard never made it off the bench.

"Oh, well," Kline said. "There's always tomorrow."

The stands emptied out, both of the schoolchildren and the scouts. Duke and Georgia Tech played next. The Blue Devils don't traditionally provide many players for the draft, and the Yellow Jackets had endured a bit of a down year. Dozens of scouts left the stadium, maybe catching a break before Miami played Clemson in a sexier matchup at night. Kline grabbed a cheeseburger from the concession stand (a "30" of a burger on the scouting scale, he said), and he and Gonzales took seats behind the plate. Who knew what they might see?

"Rizz is always on us," Kline said. "'There are big leaguers out there. You can find a big leaguer in the thirtieth round. Go do it.'"

By six p.m. he was wearing his reading glasses over his shades, checking his phone and his notes. And in front of him, a Duke pitcher named Drew Van Orden stifled Georgia Tech, taking a 6–0 lead into the bottom of the ninth. "Finish it up, big boy," Kline said. When Van Orden did, allowing five hits without a walk while striking out eight, Kline and Gonzales had added something to their file they didn't have when the day began—a senior right-hander with slightly above-average major league stuff, working his way up their draft board.

"Learned something today," Kline said. Miami and Clemson came next. The schoolkids were long gone, the stadium lights on. Another opportunity to learn something awaited.

. . .

The Nationals' war room sits on the field level of Nationals Park, down a concrete corridor from the Presidents Club and around a bend from the home clubhouse, a converted conference room that normally hosts pre- and postgame press conferences for the manager. At 8:30 p.m. on June 5, nearly two dozen Nationals staffers sat behind eight tables. The only sound came from one of the three televisions, all of which carried the first round of Major League Baseball's 2014 entry draft.

Kline and Rizzo sat at the front table, their backs facing the room. On the wall in front of them hung two whiteboards, each carefully constructed. On the left, the Nationals' top 100 choices, ranked in order of preference, each with his own magnetic card. On the right, a breakdown by position—right-handers in order, left-handers in order, infielders in order, and so on.

Kline wore a purple dress shirt and tie, and the jacket from the only suit he owns hung on the back of his chair. Folded in his wallet was a single sheet of paper, from the desk at the Courtyard by Marriott/Navy Yard. Kline and Gonzales and Zona and Baca and Costello had all been holed up there for more than a week, walking from the hotel to the war room, from the war room to the hotel, and back again (though Baca left town before the draft to attend his son's graduation from high school).

Three days before the draft, Kline scratched two names on that sheet of paper and tucked it away. He always did something like this, a test of how well he knew the draft. The Nationals picked eighteenth in the first round.

"In your mind," Kline said, "you know who you're going to take."

When Kline and the other scouts arrived May 28 in Washington, each had his own draft board in his mind. But they had to build a single list, one that would serve as their unwavering guide, not just through the first round but through forty rounds over three days. Because of that, Rizzo delivered a message before they even walked into the room: "Leave your ego at the door, and have a thick skin." Stick up for the players you believe in, but be prepared to hear push-back, and more.

"I've had guys go nose-to-nose, and we've had punches thrown," Rizzo said. "All that stuff happens."

But by the time the draft began, at seven p.m., the arguments had petered out. "Your board is your board," Kline said, and they would follow it. The entire front office filled the room—Doug Harris and Mark Scialabba from player development in one back corner, assistant general manager Bryan Minniti and director of baseball operations Adam Cromie at another back table, Gonzales alongside Harolyn Cardozo, Rizzo's take-care-of-everybody special assistant. When Arizona picked at number sixteen, there was nothing above a whisper. The only thing that separated the Nationals from their pick—the pick Kline and his staff had worked a year to make—was the Kansas City Royals. The TV screen showed an image of Art Stewart, a longtime scout with the Royals who represented the club in New York, where the draft was held.

"Whaddya got, Art?" Rizzo said, standing up. The room filled with the voice of Bud Selig, the commissioner of baseball. Selig announced that the Royals would take lefty Brandon Finnegan of Texas Christian University, then said, "The Washington Nationals have the next pick, and they are now on the clock." Before Selig finished the sentence, Rizzo was walking to a phone across the room, calling New York with his pick.

Everyone in the room knew whom the Nationals would take. But only when Selig made the announcement—Erick Fedde, a right-hander from UNLV who underwent Tommy John surgery two days earlier—did Rizzo spin around in his chair, belt out, "Very good," and begin a round of applause that briefly filled the room. Rizzo then walked over to Kline, still seated, and he rubbed the big man's shoulders.

"He doesn't sleep much, and he thinks of nothing else until the third day of the draft," Rizzo said earlier, "and then he'll collapse."

Kline eventually got up, and he fist-bumped Rizzo before he began shaking hands around the room. "Congratulations," Harris said. Cardozo, who overlooks neither a person nor a detail, began tossing ice cream sandwiches to scouts and front office members, a junior-high-style celebration. And Kline reached into his wallet for that piece of paper from the Courtyard.

The first name read "Freeland," left-hander Kyle from the University of Evansville who had gone eighth overall to the Colorado Rockies. The second name: "Fedde."

"I knew he was going to fall to us," Kline said.

Howard, the Virginia closer, went with the next pick to Cincinnati. Reed, a first-round talent in Kline's mind, fell— but not far enough for the Nationals, because Houston took him with the first pick of the second round. The next day, in the fifth round, with the 154th pick in the draft, the Nationals took Duke right-hander Drew Van Orden.

And on Sunday, Kline flew home to Phoenix. He watched a movie on the way, and said he'd decompress for a week. He was kidding himself.

"I won't be able to," he said. "I get too stir-crazy."

So the plan was to see the Nationals' minor league games at all levels, where he would watch the kids he drafted in years past and have the chance to evaluate his own work. Then an endless list of games, the Cape Cod League—an elite summer league where college kids become accustomed to wooden bats—and the Area Code Games, a showcase for the best high school players, and on and on. The 2015 draft was almost exactly a year off. The work, though, begins anew, because there's another flight to be boarded, another car to be rented, another player to be seen. Always.

PITCHER DOUG FISTER

The Starter

At 8:32 p.m. on a sweltering Wednesday night in July, Doug Fister stood on the rubber atop the mound at Nationals Park and wound up for the eightieth time. His 6-foot-8 frame unfurled as it had all evening—hands together over his head quickly, left foot striding downhill toward the plate, two-seam fastball tumbling at the hitter lower and lower and lower, constantly lower. Tyler Matzek, the opposing pitcher for the Colorado Rockies, stared at the 1-2 sinker as it went by, and when the home-plate umpire rang him up, Matzek walked to one dugout, Fister to the other, done for the day.

"A constant battle all night," Fister said later, sighing, standing in front of his locker, his uniform pants replaced by checked surfer shorts, his spikes by flip-flops. After that pitch to Matzek, Nationals manager Matt Williams lifted Fister for a pinch hitter. His start was over, his public work complete. At 9:45 p.m., he strode through the clubhouse, shook hands with fellow right-hander Tanner Roark, and walked out the doors into the stark gray concourse. A bus hummed, waiting to pick up the Rockies and take them to the airport. Fister's brain hummed along with it. The process of forgetting everything that had just happened—seven innings, seven hits, eighty pitches, a gut-punch of a three-run homer, plenty of mistakes even though it all made for a 4–3 victory—began.

"I have until the time the game is over and I walk out of the clubhouse to be mad," Fister said. "As soon as I walk out that door, I flush whatever's happened."

For the ten Nationals position players and two relievers who played that night against the Rockies, the flush is a nightly process, because another game almost always looms the next day. The potential to extend a scalding streak or a slump is rarely more than twenty-four hours removed.

For starting pitchers, the process is slower, mixing patience with intensity, downtime with diligence. A position player's existence is metronomic, with no one day more important than another. A starter's is a series of crescendos, each building to a special public performance. In a 162-game season, a healthy starter, in the modern game, will pitch a maximum of 35 times. That gives each 127 games in which he is all but guaranteed not to play. Decent work, with every weekend four days long, right?

"Four days off is not four days off," Nationals pitching coach Steve McCatty said, and he knows, because he made 161 starts in the majors himself.

So when Fister left the mound in the middle of the game against the Rockies, he accepted his high fives and fist bumps in the dugout, grabbed some water, then headed to the comfort of the clubhouse to try to find comfort in his mind. He had begun the game poorly, leaving too many pitches up in the strike zone, including the cutter that Rockies catcher Michael McKenry deposited over the left-field fence in the second, a devastating three-run homer.

"You're so emotional, you can't look at the game objectively," Fister said. "I like to be completely—and a lot of times *brutally*—honest with myself. And it's hard right after the game."

He had already been to the clubhouse between innings, filling his ears with country music, walking the line between being focused on and overcome by the game. But with the final two innings playing out, and the outcome still in doubt, Fister moved past his locker to the training room. The Nationals' radio broadcast pumped through the speakers, the television on the wall showed Tyler Clippard coming on in relief. But in the moments after Fister's body had exhausted itself with one start, after his mind grappled with the good and the bad, he had to get ready for the next.

"That starts the five-day process of building back up," Fister said. "It starts right then."

. . .

T his was not always second nature. Growing up in the central California town of Merced, Fister wasn't programmed as a pitcher, a starter. He was an athlete—baseball, soccer, cross-country. He ran so much the neighborhood kids called him Forrest Gump. As he sprouted to 6 feet 8 inches, he played basketball. When he was originally selected in the baseball draft, it was as a first baseman.

"I try not to be a robot," Fister said. Yet his professional existence calls for some physical and mental robotics, repetitive, regimented actions. Fister's mind naturally scurries about; he describes his style as borderline OCD—obsessive-compulsive disorder. As he played two years in community college and later at Fresno State, he had plenty of places to put his thoughts. If he wasn't pitching, he was hitting. If he wasn't hitting, he was fielding. He might catch a bullpen session for another pitcher. He might take fly balls in the outfield. There was always something.

But his senior year, he decided to concentrate on pitching. He was selected in the seventh round of the draft by the Seattle Mariners, who immediately sent him to Class A Everett, Washington. Suddenly, there was no batting practice to take, no college classes, no first baseman's mitt. Here, the life of a starting pitcher sank in.

"It was kind of, 'What do I do with myself?'" he said.

That question has been asked for years. Only in the past decade and a half has the answer become so refined.

"We didn't have video," said McCatty, whose career with the Oakland Athletics spanned from 1977 to 1985. "We didn't have weights. There's a lot more breaking down first-pitch swings, what they hit in what count, what they hit off what pitch. The numbers are all there for pretty much anything you want to find."

But before you can find that, you have to find yourself. Fister struggled with that in those early days of the minors, and it affected his preparation. He made just four starts for Everett before concerns about a high pitch count over the entirety of the college and pro seasons sent him to the bullpen. He returned to the rotation the next year, but posted a 5.02 ERA over two full seasons at Class AA. His struggles infuriated him, and for two or three days after starts, he would fume. There was a new weight program, a new running program, shoulder maintenance, a throwing program.

"Especially at the lower levels of the minor leagues," Fister said, "you're really trying to learn how to get through each five-day rotation."

Even when he got to the majors with the Mariners, in 2009, he had to figure out those four days in between. What do I do with my brain? What do I do with my body? For generations, there has been no uniform response. Steve Carlton turned to martial arts. Roger Clemens ran. Randy Johnson became a weight-room resident. Curt Schilling developed into a bookworm, knowing hitters better than they knew themselves.

"It's something that . . . to each his own," Nationals right-hander Stephen Strasburg said. "Some guys don't like to do that much, just recover. Some guys like to train really hard. At first, I probably over-trained a little bit, and it kind of just caught up to me as the season went on."

However it's handled, it must be productive. "It's not a vacation," Strasburg said. And so it is that while his team-mates continued their tussle with the Rockies, Doug Fister grabbed a large rubber band used to offer resistance and began working the same right shoulder that had just unloaded those 80 pitches.

For Nationals' starters, there is no chiseled-in-stone routine in those moments after they leave the mound, but head athletic trainer Lee Kuntz is adamant that they work their throwing arms, particularly when they are already in distress right after they pitch. This is done in March or May with September and October in mind, and it is often done when the game is still going on. A pitcher's long-term health is more important than whether he sees his teammates record the final out.

As the Rockies game played on, Fister immediately went to work with the set of rubber bands, providing resistance for his arm, putting further workload on an already tired shoulder.

"A lot of people will say, 'You're beating a dead issue; he's tired,'" Kuntz said. "*Yes*. But if they had a huge workload, we can drastically reduce what they do in the training room, and they still get their routine and the discipline of having to do it when they're tired. It's a little nugget for me. The idea is to get the monkey to jump through the hoop and think it's his idea."

For Fister, this isn't a problem. The OCD part of him dictates that he relishes the work immediately after he pitches; he understands its importance over the next five days, over the rest of the season. Kuntz and the training staff frequently have pitchers submerge in a cool tub after pitching and work their arms that way, using the water as resistance. They will ice their arms, making them look something like a half Hulk, with one side of their upper bodies wrapped in Ace bandages and ice bags, because that can calm swelling. And if Kuntz is able to diagnose real fatigue, he can suggest to McCatty that the workload in coming days be reduced.

But even with that close monitoring, by both himself and the Nationals' athletic training staff, Fister woke up the day after his start against Colorado feeling sore. "Just mentally, physically exhausted," he said. It is like this for every major league starter after every major league start. "You can feel it," Roark said.

Fister's response, at seven a.m.: a four-and-a-half-mile run with his fiancée. This is nothing more than cleansing. They were training for a half marathon together, so they took to the hills in northern Virginia, talked about the houses they passed by that had been put on the market, watched a squirrel run in front of them. Even as a kid, only two things could truly wipe Fister's brain clean: mowing the lawn and running.

"It's a mental and physical break for me," Fister said. "I use the mental side of things just to clear my mind and enjoy nature."

The Nationals actually had the day after Fister's start off completely, the last scheduled off day before the all-star break, so he, his fiancée, and some friends from out of town toured the monuments and the National Mall that morning. When the Chicago Cubs arrived for a weekend series beginning on the Fourth of July, Fister began his typical at-the-ballpark day-after routine: an hour and a half to two hours in the weight room, training his upper body and his core, a light game of catch out to maybe 100 or 120 feet to get blood flowing in his arm, then shagging balls during batting practice, reminding himself that "if it's the seventeenth inning, and we're out of players, Skip might need someone to run out there."

For most starters, the second day of work after pitching is reserved for a bullpen session. Strasburg, in his early days, would fire 50 or 60 pitches on those days, trying to refine every little thing. He has since toned that down, and each of the Nationals' starters now has settled into a comfort zone of somewhere between 20 and 35 pitches, give or take. Each starter except Fister.

"I'm so particular in my pitching style and my bullpens that if it's not where I want it to be, either one, I'm not happy with it, or two, I'm going to continue to throw until I get it," he said. "And a lot of times, I don't get it that day. So I'm just continually pounding my head against a wall."

Early in his career, these bullpen sessions became completely counterproductive. After as many as 75 pitches, he was physically spent and mentally frayed. So now, he is the rarest of major league starting pitchers: He doesn't throw a bullpen between starts. Rather, two days after he pitches, he plays a hard game of catch from about sixty feet away, but not from a mound, to a squatting catcher.

"They don't have to do anything they don't want to," McCatty said. "I can suggest things, but it's up to them."

It is a nod to starters' individuality, to their internal quirks and preferences. On the morning of the second day of the series against the Cubs, after he had worked on his legs in the weight room, Fister retreated to the grass in right field at Nationals Park and began his most strenuous on-field activity between starts. Like everything in his routine, this workout is meticulously dissected. He wears sneakers instead of spikes because that forces him to keep his weight on his back foot to avoid slipping on the grass. If he stays back, he can properly separate his lower body from his upper body, getting the former in proper position so he can follow through with the latter, perfectly timed.

But in the course of the session, Fister also threw balls from all angles—sidearm, 45 degrees, a bit on the run. Again, this is by design.

"I want to do it all as a shortstop," Fister said. "On the mound, the arm slightly changes its arm slot due to timing issues of where your body is, where your feet are, fatigue. There's a lot of outside influences that have their effect on me on the mound, so I'm trying to be more athletic."

This throwing session serves another purpose: The aches from the previous start are fully expunged. The next start is just two days away.

"Now," he said, "I have a new target."

When Fister got to the ballpark for his third day of work following his start against Colorado, there was still a bit of research to be tackled. The Rockies scalded several balls over the course of those seven innings, but Fister also fixed the problem, eventually. He retired eleven of the final twelve men he faced, and McKenry's homer provided Colorado its only runs.

"I didn't make [an adjustment] in one pitch, and I didn't make it right out of the gates," Fister said. "But I finally made it, and it was enough to get the team the win."

So when he arrived on that Sunday, he sought only confirmation of what he suspected, and he turned to video. For such a tall pitcher, Fister's windup is remarkably compact: hands rapidly and tightly over his head, stride not particularly long, ball on top of the hitter before he knows it. The entire operation is efficient by design, so much so that, at that point in July, opposing base runners had attempted just one steal against him all season—and that runner was thrown out.

When Fister arrived following an offseason trade with Detroit, he told McCatty one key to his success is that he must work quickly. He needs his rhythm. It's why he listens to music before, and even during, his starts.

"I'm a terrible dancer," Fister said. "I don't have any rhythm. But that's how I kind of keep a pace on the mound."

Against the Rockies, he lost his rhythm. He slowed down. "Hurry it up," McCatty told him between innings. And when he sat in front of two television images—one showing slices of his eight shutout innings against Atlanta in June, the other his seven spotty innings against Colorado—he could see the difference. In two days, he was due to start against Baltimore. If he expected to succeed, the video would have to look more like the confident, eager pitcher against the Braves, not the timid, lagging pitcher from the first few innings of the Rockies game.

"If my tempo's too slow, my upper body starts floating forward, my ball gets up," he said, "and it starts getting out of whack."

He left the park that day feeling better about his prospects. "He's so cerebral in his approach," said Williams. When Fister arrived the next day, the Orioles were in town, and his preparation took another step. In spring training, as he learned about Fister the pitcher and the person, Williams thought he might be a good fit in the Nationals' defensive meetings, which take place on the first day of each new series. There, Mark Weidemaier, the Nationals' defensive coordinator and advance coach, lays out the tendencies of each opposing hitter and how each player should position himself on the field. Because Fister doesn't overwhelm hitters, relying on a steady 88-mph sinker, Williams thought he might be willing to contribute to a more holistic approach to defense.

"He's going to make the opposing team put the ball in play, so he wants us to understand what his plan is so we can develop our own plan to defend it," Williams said. "Pretty simple stuff, but it oftentimes goes unnoticed or un-talked-about."

So Fister and the Nationals' position players discussed how to pitch Nelson Cruz, how to pitch Adam Jones, how to pitch Chris Davis. An American Leaguer his whole career until joining the Nationals, Fister had faced the Orioles six times previously, including three times in Camden Yards. His presence in the meeting meant the Nationals' defense would be coordinated, more like football, where all eleven defensive players are following the same plan instead of the middle linebacker calling one play and the defenders around him running another.

"I wish they all did it," Weidemaier said. "But some guys aren't able to handle all of that information. He's a guy that can process it."

That afternoon, when the Nationals took batting practice, Fister ran in the outfield, chasing balls. He sprinted for thirty or forty feet at a time, the last bit of physical work, bursts to keep his legs alive. When the game began, he climbed onto the top bench in the Nationals' dugout and watched each Orioles hitter. He leaned over to backup catcher Jose Lobaton, sitting to his left.

"He'll tell you," Lobaton said, "'If you're playing tomorrow, this is what we're going to do.'"

At 3:35 p.m. on July 9, Fister walked through the visitors' clubhouse at Camden Yards still wearing shorts and sneakers. He not only didn't pitch the previous day, as scheduled, but didn't even warm up, because rain washed out the game at Nationals Park. The two teams would move their series to Baltimore the next day, so as soon as the announcement of a postponement was made in Washington, Fister was in Williams's office: "What's the plan?"

"It can't have any effect," Fister said.

Some starters are notoriously cranky on the days they pitch, some downright unapproachable. Fister, serious but congenial, prefers to think of himself as the same person be it day one or day five in this cycle. Yet regardless of the pitcher and his personal approach, he is almost always playing the game in his mind before he plays it on the field. "You're seeing it and seeing it and seeing it and seeing it," McCatty said. "And seeing it. I couldn't sleep."

Fister's plan for visualization is the opposite. By 3:55 p.m., he had tucked a pair of yellow buds in his ears, pulled on a red sweatshirt, yanked the hood over his eyes, and unfolded his frame on one of the four black couches that sit in the center of the clubhouse. "Get comfy, Doug," lefty Ross Detwiler said, smiling. By now they all knew what was coming: Fister's pregame nap. He has pulled this off on a chair in front of his locker. He has dozed under a training table. But he always sleeps. First, for rest. Second, to get his heart rate down. And third, in a subconscious way, to execute his pitches and dissect the Orioles.

"I go through all the mental points of what I do—how this foot needs to land, what I need to feel off my fingertips, how do I finish," he said. "I'm constantly playing off what I do well."

When Fister fell asleep, the iPhone resting on his chest filling his ears with the Tim McGraw channel from Pandora, the Tigers and Dodgers played quietly on the clubhouse TVs. When he sat up forty minutes later, Germany and the Netherlands pushed each other in a World Cup match.

It wasn't until 6:35 p.m., with the game a half hour off,

that Fister arrived in the visitors' bullpen in left-center field, pulled his glove from his belt—where he had tucked it under his sweatshirt—and placed a bottle of water on the mound. He returned to the outfield, stretched by himself, took a ball from McCatty, and began playing catch. After five minutes, when he and Wilson Ramos, the starting catcher that night, returned to the bullpen, Fister bent back each of the five fingers on his right hand, then each of the five on his left.

"If you're going to maximize your output," Fister said, "you've got to take care of each individual little muscle and make sure that everything is taken care of."

To warm up, he began with a fastball on the inside corner to a right-handed hitter, then worked the other side of the plate. After nine fastballs, he threw two curves. After twenty-one pitches from the windup and nine more from the stretch, he stepped back and took a drink. There's no telling how many gallons of water and Gatorade he takes in on the two days leading up to his start. He grabbed a towel draped over McCatty's shoulder to wipe his face.

"If I don't have a good bullpen session out there, I need to reevaluate and make the adjustment," Fister said. "It should be just a time to get loose. But if it's not working, I need to revamp my game plan and really just make sure they start swinging the bat."

After six more pitches, Fister was done, bumping fists with McCatty and bullpen coach Matt LeCroy. "Not too bad," Fister said later. He then took the sweaty towel that had been tossed over McCatty's shoulder and folded it neatly, as if stacking shirts for a department store display, and placed it on the bench.

"He likes things just right," Lobaton said.

By quirks of both schedule and weather, Fister hadn't pitched in a game for a week. Nearly all the intervening time had built toward this moment.

"It doesn't matter who's in the box," Fister said. "It's a matter of: I need to take care of my business and be ready to go."

The arm exercises, the running, the weights, the video, the treatment, the nap: They all determined whether, in fact, he would be ready. And at 7:24 p.m., Doug Fister walked up the back of the mound at Camden Yards, kicked at the rubber, adjusted his hat, and unleashed his first pitch—everything for which he had prepared.

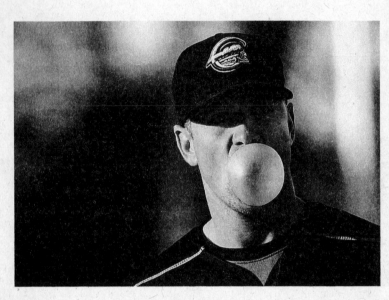

TYLER MOORE

The Twenty-sixth
Man

The lights flickered at McCoy Stadium in Pawtucket, Rhode Island, and by this point, after 10:15 p.m., the grainy shadows had long since been established. In the majors, the sheer wattage—so many bulbs on so many giant towers—obliterates even the slightest chance of shade on the field. Here, in the International League, Tyler Moore stepped into the batter's box, and hazy images of his 6-foot-2 frame fell in the dirt around him.

This was the top of the ninth, down a run, man on, cleanup hitter at the plate. At Nationals Park, it's what baseball players live for. At McCoy Stadium, they have to stave off the reality of their lives. "You don't get the goose bumps here," said Ryan Mattheus, Moore's teammate with the Syracuse Chiefs.

Moore had been in this very spot in the majors, with the Nationals—shoot, in the *playoffs*. But this was late July in the International League. Even the 9,397 who showed up for Ladies' Night—why not, when each woman got a long-stemmed rose?—drifted out into the parking lots. Had this been Boston versus Washington, the ballpark would have hummed. This was Pawtucket versus Syracuse. Moore's shadows danced in the dirt as he took a warm-up cut.

"This is our livelihood," he said later. "This counts."

In the summer of 2014, Moore was twenty-seven, and his native Mississippi fell from his lips with every "Yes, sir" and "No, ma'am." He was an American home owner newly married to his high school sweetheart. He was doing exactly what he wanted to do far from where he wanted to be. It is the essence of Triple A baseball.

"The hardest level for personalities," said Randy Knorr, the Nationals bench coach who once managed the team's top minor league franchise. "No one wants to be there. No one thinks they should be there."

And yet here Moore stood, digging into the box in the ninth inning, finding focus. He had done the same in the big leagues—427 times over the past three years. As a rookie in 2012, he smacked 10 homers and stayed on the roster through a run to a division title, a promising piece of a post-season team.

"Felt like I was never gonna go back down," he said. "You discover: You do."

And then, if you're one of the dozens of players like Moore across the major and minor leagues, you go back up. And you come back down. Then you . . . well, try to keep your sanity. Moore's home is in Madison, Mississippi, but for the season he lived at the Staybridge Suites in tiny Liverpool, New York, outside Syracuse, three miles from his home office, NBT Bank Stadium. In Washington, he relied on the kindness of Nationals first baseman Adam LaRoche, who let him stay in a small apartment in his house. When he'd be in either place, no one really knew.

"You pretty much become a professional at packing and unpacking," Moore said. In his current professional existence, Moore must stay ready for his next game, his next at-bat. He must also stay ready for his next phone call, his next flight to meet the major league team, putting disappointment and frustration in a box somewhere, lid shut tight. In the shadows, he must somehow focus on possibility and opportunity.

Twice that year he had been called up to the Nationals. Twice he had been sent back down. If the major league life brings a grinding rhythm that wears on the hearts and minds and bodies of even star players, at least it comes with charter flights and checks with all those zeroes. In the minors, the everydayness is the same. The payoff is not.

Moore dug in against Pawtucket Red Sox closer Heath Hembree.

"In a big league game in that situation, there's thirty or

forty thousand people, especially if we're trying to win the division," Moore said, sitting outside the team hotel in downtown Providence, midnight approaching, a breeze cooling him off. "There's gonna be . . ." and he trailed off, eyes distant, and managed a chuckle.

"If we're in Washington playing the Braves, there's gonna be some pressure there," he said. "Here? You just try to stay focused on: Be small at the plate, think simple, and just try to come through for the team."

Seven hours earlier, in the visitors' clubhouse that same day, the small stereo set up on the floor in a corner blared an endless string of country hits, Luke Bryan and Jason Aldean strumming out the sound track of minor league life. On the television screen above, Nationals reliever Drew Storen took the ball in the ninth inning of a game in Miami. Two card games held at separate tables sputtered to a slower pace. Eyes darted to the screen, then back at the cards, then back to the screen again.

"I consider a lot of those guys good friends," Moore said, looking at the Nationals game. Wherever he has been, he prides himself on being a good teammate. That could be in Washington, where his job has mostly been to sit to the side and learn, a bit player. Here, it was to play first base and bat fourth, a key cog.

Either place, he must hit, which is essentially all he has

ever done since he signed with the Nationals as a sixteenth-round draft pick from Mississippi State in 2008. That year, he was handed the schedule for the Vermont Expos, then Washington's entry in the short-season Class A New York–Penn League. It showed 77 games in 80 days. He laughed.

"A lot of guys coming out of college, they don't know how to fail yet," Moore said. "This game is really all about failure, and just trying to handle it and understanding how to get yourself back when you do."

Back then, he had no clue about any of it. Guys in the low minors, they're all on the rise. They look at the major league roster and wonder where they might fit, even when such a prospect is several years and countless organizational decisions away. "The biggest lesson down here," said Syracuse manager Billy Gardner Jr., who has managed at every level in the minors, "is control the controllables."

But the major league team that played on the screen in the visitors' clubhouse—well, when you're at Class AAA, you're one tweaked hamstring away. Each player at each locker stall, the guys strewn on two couches, those peeking up from their card games, they all knew it. On April 6, it was snowing in Syracuse. The Chiefs had played one game of their season. With the Nationals, reserve outfielder Scott Hairston went down with an oblique strain. Moore got the call: Get to Washington.

"There's nothing like your first time," Moore said, "but it's always exciting."

That first time came two years earlier, when Moore was in Syracuse with all the credentials. He hit 31 homers and drove in 111 runs in 2010 for Class A Potomac, slugged 31 more homers in 2011 for Class AA Harrisburg. He was blowing through the minors. Late the next April, Tony Beasley, then the Syracuse manager, called him at one a.m. He had to be in Los Angeles the next day. Dodger Stadium. The majors.

"That was stressful, but in the best way," Moore said. No sleep, two flights, deciphering the taxis at LAX. He got a hit in his first major league game. He became a starter because of injuries. When he hit his first two major league homers in mid-June in Toronto, the Nationals sat in first place, and Moore told reporters: "It just keeps getting better. It's a fun place to be."

The next season, he made the team out of spring training. And in his first 95 at-bats—sporadic plate appearances as a pinch hitter, a fill-in starter—he hit .158. "Your skills don't diminish," Knorr said. "But you don't get to do it enough." It's the Triple A conundrum: Play every day in the minors and find a rhythm, or stay in the majors and face inordinate pressure with each at-bat, because there's no telling when the next one might come.

Moore was sent to Syracuse. In a way, he was introduced to his current life.

"You can make all the excuses in the world, but it doesn't make it any better," Moore said. "It's just like, 'Hey, you know what? This is the best thing for me. I need to go down here and get my confidence back and get some at-bats, and find out what was going on.'"

Back when he was in Class A, at Potomac—a short drive down I-95 from Nationals Park—Moore began figuring out that every minor league season would bring both success and struggle, some of each for sustained periods. At the all-star break, he was hitting .190. "For two months," he said, "I just lost it."

So he took to writing in a journal during whatever hot streak he could find. "I wanted to be specific," he said. What did he feel like at the plate? Where were his hands? His head? His feet? What did he do before the games? Then, when things turned sour, he had a touchstone.

"The more that you can kind of hang on to the good things, then I feel like the more successful you'll be for a longer period of time," he said.

He had his journal with him in Pawtucket. He had it in Washington, where he stayed for a month in the spring, started five times, hit .200, and was sent back down. Five days later, the Nationals put LaRoche on the disabled list with a strained quadriceps. Moore was back on a flight, meeting the team in Oakland. By the end of May, he was sent back to Syracuse. By the middle of summer, he hadn't been back to the majors, his life a series of nights at the Staybridge, breakfasts with teammates at the American Diner, calls back home to his bride, bus rides through the night from Pawtucket to Scranton and back to Syracuse, six a.m.

commercial flights for longer trips—with games that night. Charters? Pffffft.

"You have to keep your head down," Moore said. "There's no other way to do it. You have to keep working hard."

On the television screen, Storen got the final Marlin to hit into a fielder's choice, and the Nationals clung to a narrow victory. Moore, still in shorts, went into a corner and grabbed a black bat, slipped two white gloves onto his hands, walked past the refrigerator with the ketchup and the relish and the Coffee-mate, and headed to the batting cage beneath the stands to begin his work.

As the Chiefs finished their batting-practice session at McCoy that evening, the view from their dugout suddenly became cluttered with clipboards lowered on strings by early-arriving fans in the seats above. There were sheets for specific players, baseball cards encased in plastic, each with a Sharpie attached.

"I already signed this one," Mattheus said as he looked at his clipboard. "That's what happens when you're thirty and you're still in Triple A," and he scribbled his name on another card.

Class AAA is something of baseball's halfway house. Seven of the players in the Chiefs' starting lineup that night had been to the majors. None wanted to return here. McCoy Stadium is a patchwork of eighty billboards in the outfield. In between innings, two stuffed bears aim a T-shirt gun at the crowd. The version of "God Bless America" is taped. And in between it all, the players try to work.

"Guys there are fighting for their lives in the game of professional baseball," said Doug Harris, the Nationals' vice president of player development, who oversees the farm system. "It's a very interesting mix."

Each player involved in the mix has considered his situation carefully, either by curiosity or necessity or both. Moore knew 2014 was the last season in which the Nationals could "option" him to the minor leagues as many times as they want. It is a fact on which he does not want to dwell. Typically, players have three option years. After that, a player must be exposed to other teams—who could claim him—before he passes to the minors. In 2015, there would be no shuttle between Syracuse and Washington for Moore, because some other team would certainly pick him up, give him a chance.

"It pops into your head every once in a while," Moore said. "But you can't think about it."

Yet it's an inevitable battle, an individual battle. Some players can't help but obsess with the entire roster at every level of the organization—who has how many options remaining, who is performing poorly in the majors, whom they might replace. They know so much. The major league minimum salary is $500,000, and players make a prorated version of that for each day in the majors. Typical Class AAA salaries are around $2,100 per month, though some minor league free agents can earn $60,000 to $70,000 for a season. All those numbers dance through heads, which can be crippling.

"For young guys, it's very hard," said Greg Dobbs, a thirty-six-year-old first baseman for the Chiefs who had nearly 2,100 major league at-bats over parts of eleven seasons. "They can't think that way. That's when you can see the wheels start turning and they start showing their frustration outwardly. They may say or do things that are out of character. But that's why they're doing it. They don't know how to handle that, and they can't quite grasp it. They haven't been through it."

So as the Nationals traded for Hairston in 2013 and signed veteran outfielder Nate McLouth in the offseason, Moore had no control. The organization was replacing his potential with known quantities, guys who have proven they could handle part-time roles year after year. Something similar has happened to almost every player on the Syracuse roster. In the spring, right-handed reliever Aaron Barrett blew away opposing hitters and, in turn, the Nationals' front office. He made the majors for the first time. The collateral damage: Mattheus, who helped the Nationals to the playoffs in 2012, pounded his fist into his locker in a pique of frustration in 2013—breaking his hand—and hadn't reestablished himself in the big leagues.

"It's human nature to play GM," Mattheus said. "We all

see the rosters. We all kind of know where we stand. We're all biased in our own eyes."

Mattheus had had two four-day stints in the majors in 2014. In four appearances, he didn't give up a run. Each time, he was sent back down because someone else returned from injury. The first time, he stormed out of manager Matt Williams's office. Syracuse? Again?

"I had the poor-me attitude," he said. "I had the it-should-be-me-up-there thinking. And it's sad to say, but I almost looked at it as: 'I'm better than this. I shouldn't be here.' I almost threw away a month and a half of my season because of that. . . .

"It can happen to a whole clubhouse. The popular thing to say is 'We should all be there.' So if we're all negative, we all kind of feel comfortable being negative around each other. It's a vicious cycle."

Thus, the most delicate and significant of Harris's daily tasks can be monitoring the mental state of some six minor league teams simultaneously. "Such an underrated part of the job," Harris said. But it's obvious: The Nationals can't have players giving away six weeks of their seasons because they're mad at the organization for perceived slights.

"More often than not," Harris said, "these are difficult conversations."

And yet Moore, even at the low points, has made it easy. "He set every record we had," said Jeff McClaskey, Moore's coach at Northwest Rankin High, "and he was humble the whole way." The son of a school principal and a nurse who grew up in the county seat of Brandon, Mississippi, Moore is, Harris said, "the consummate professional. He has unbelievable class as a player and a man."

"Just always try to see the good in things," Moore said. "Sometimes, this world can be hard."

He said this sitting outside the Hilton Providence, his bed beckoning. His wife was nearly 1,400 miles away, tending to her job and their house—to their lives, of which he's a part just half the year. "If there was any security," he said, "she'd be here." But there isn't, so she's not. The next day's game started at noon.

When Moore took his spot in the batter's box against Hembree, Chiefs outfielder Steven Souza was on first base. Moore already had a double, and here was his chance to tie up a game on a July night in a dank neighborhood on the outskirts of Providence.

Two seasons earlier, the Nationals trailed by a run in the first postseason game in franchise history. Men were on second and third in the eighth. And then-manager Davey Johnson called on Moore to pinch-hit.

"Biggest at-bat of my life," he said. Facing Cardinals left-hander Marc Rzepczynski, Moore flared a single into right field that scored Michael Morse to tie and Ian Desmond to take the lead. The Nationals won.

Here, in July in Pawtucket, such moments can't be created from thin air. Hembree didn't play along anyway, and Moore laid off four straight pitches, drawing a walk. Brandon Laird, the next hitter, flied out to end it, and Moore jogged into the dugout, then walked into the clubhouse, which was dead quiet even fifteen minutes later. Players sifted over what's considered the best spread in the International League, on this night beef tips or baked scrod, broccoli, and loaded baked potatoes. A fridge stocked with a few Bud Lights and Coors Lights went untouched. At any level, a loss is a loss.

"You just try to process your night," Moore said. "You think about the pitches you wish you wouldn't have swung at, happy about the pitches you got a hit on that you did swing at. But you can't dwell on it. When I leave here, it has to be gone."

He shuffled to the shower. At 9:30 a.m. the next day, he was back at the park, back in this room, back with these guys, back playing cards, back taking a few cuts in the batting cage under the stands. Moore has also taken to the Chiefs' Bible study, which draws on his roots in Mississippi in the church.

"Sometimes, you get sent down, and it's just discouraging, and you try to figure out some of the pieces to it," Moore said. "You just get lost. You're trying to understand why everything's going on, and a lot of times, I just read the Word, and it really helps out. It's the rock."

The other rock, though, is one another. It is, above all

else, what minor leaguers have. No one else has tasted what they've tasted—the hotels, the food, the money, the crowds, the intensity—and then been forced to eat gruel for months at a time. The Chiefs play Ping-Pong in their home clubhouse. The visitors' clubhouse at McCoy has a foosball table, and it saw action. The card games, the breakfasts, the saying "Hey" to guys you saw just hours before—it makes it all tolerable.

"Whatever it takes to stay sane," Moore said.

Two boxes of Dunkin' Donuts sat on a table across the clubhouse. The MLB Network squawked from the television, news of the trade deadline, something that could have affected anyone in that room. Zach Walters, an infielder with the Chiefs called up to the Nationals earlier in the month, was dealt to Cleveland. "Crazy," Moore said.

Yet he didn't know whether he'd be there the following year. LaRoche, the man most directly blocking his path, was a free agent, but Ryan Zimmerman looked likely to take over at first base. The outfield had Bryce Harper, Denard Span, Jayson Werth. Where would that leave Moore?

"I've said for a couple of years I would love to see him get traded," LaRoche said. "Selfishly I want him here, because I like being around him. But this guy could be an impact player playing every day for somebody. It's just a bad situation here."

Moore doesn't see it that way. "The Nationals is like a family," he said at his locker. "Can't really imagine leaving."

In August, though, Souza got called up for his major league debut. When Souza got hurt, the Nationals brought up outfielder Michael Taylor.

And Moore kept showing up for work, kept hitting. The International League regular season would end September 1—the day major league rosters can expand—and the first-place Chiefs may well have the playoffs after that.

Yet those aren't the playoffs about which any of the Chiefs truly care. The Nationals, too, sat in first place. What would Tyler Moore give for one more call to get on that shuttle, for another chance to stick in the bigs?

"It's where we all want to be," he said, and at 3:30 p.m., he walked past the minor league spread of chicken and green beans into the minor league showers, full of major league hopes.

ROB McDONALD (*RIGHT*) WITH JAYSON WERTH

The Glue

Three buses filled the concourse outside the home clubhouse at Nationals Park, visible to only a few security guards and those who would climb aboard for the ride to Union Station, for the train to New York, for the games in Queens, for the flight to Atlanta and on and on, not to return for eleven days. It was two minutes before eight p.m. on a Wednesday in September, and the whiteboard inside the clubhouse—where attendants swept away the last bit of detritus from that day's game—was red-letter clear about what followed: *BUS 8:10.* But all the meal money hadn't yet been given out, so Rob McDonald remained behind his desk in his office, just at the top of the stairs that lead down to the home dugout.

The players came out randomly, each grabbing an

envelope, each heading to the players' bus. By 8:02 p.m., General Manager Mike Rizzo took the first seat in the first row of the staff bus, just under the red sign that flashed "Watch Your Step," just behind the driver, just across from Manager Matt Williams, just in front of twenty-nine other Nationals employees, none of them players, each with a role. As the clock ticked toward departure time, McDonald gathered two of the three bus drivers just outside the door.

Williams likes the players to depart the buses first, to board the train or plane before the coaches and the staff. So for McDonald, it mattered which bus pulled in where. It mattered which door opened when. There are no small jobs.

"Perfect," McDonald said, message delivered. "Thank you, guys."

McDonald climbed the steps and took his seat across from Mike Wallace, the bespectacled, omnipresent figure known forever as Wally. Nine hours earlier, Wallace stood outside the Nationals' clubhouse, clipboard in hand, watching as a mountain of black suitcases grew higher and higher, seven luggage racks obscuring the sign on the wall commemorating the 2012 National League East Division Championship. Wallace and his staff helped load those bags onto a truck, which drove during that afternoon's game against the Atlanta Braves. When the Nationals arrived at their Madison Avenue hotel, they would go to their rooms, and their bags would be there, waiting. Wallace and McDonald have a goal: When players bring their luggage to spring training, they shouldn't have to pick it up again until the fall, until after the last out.

"They should forget how heavy their bags are," McDonald said.

A baseball season, stretching from the tail of one winter to the cusp of the next, erodes the bodies and minds of the men who play. How they handle those demands can determine their performance, there for the world to see nearly every single day.

What's not plain to the eye is what gets them to that position. The Nationals, from the lowest levels of the minors to the major league team, control some 200 players, the stars of the show. Yet they employ more than 1,100 people who never get an at-bat or throw a pitch, whose names are never known. Rank them in importance, top to bottom, and Rizzo—who constructs the roster and oversees the entire operation—would be up there, as would Williams, who runs the games. Not far behind, though, would be McDonald and Wallace, whose titles—vice president of clubhouse operations, and team travel and clubhouse and equipment manager, respectively—seem nebulous. Their missions are all-encompassing and essential.

"Picture this team as a band," McDonald said. "I'm kind of the tour manager. I kind of oversee everything. I make sure we go in the right direction, try to troubleshoot, try to make sure the people who are involved with the band are happy, and they can put on the best show possible."

"I tell people that if someone came in here naked, they could go out and play baseball fully equipped outside in front of a crowd," Wallace said. "Basically, we want to make it so that the only thing the player has to worry about is performing on the field, and that anything and everything else that they need—that we take care of it and make sure that they have it."

None of the Nationals' 33 flights or 2 train trips or 5 bus charters over the course of the season would happen without either of them. "Guys like that? More important than your seventh-inning reliever," said Braves manager Fredi Gonzalez, who recommended McDonald for his first big league job. The last of the Nationals' 12 road trips would go through 3 cities and involve 1 train ride, 3 flights, 46 bus rides, 78 passengers, 25 equipment trunks, 6 sets of golf clubs, 70 equipment bags, 1 massage table, 125 pieces of luggage, including 2 guitars. What could go wrong?

"There's always something," Wallace said.

It is their job to take each something seriously but casually, urgently but in control. McDonald's memo of guidelines for how the clubhouse and travel staff should conduct itself includes, among the 14 points, "develop a high level of concentration" and "be quick, but not in a hurry." Each task, however esoteric, must be handled professionally. Jayson Werth needs a microwave in his hotel room in New York? Check. Drew Storen forgot to put in his request to leave tickets for his family? No problem. Steven Souza needs to find a place to work on his Chevy? Rob's got a guy. Someone needs a button sewn on the shirt he intends to wear on the road trip? Wally has his needle and thread at the ready. Rookie outfielder Michael Taylor needs a place in New York to quietly get a meal? Done.

"He's got to deal with twenty-five prima donnas that get paid a lot of money that want everything that they want," veteran Ryan Zimmerman said of McDonald, "and he's got to make them all happy. That can't be easy."

When the staff bus pulled into Union Station at 8:25 that night, McDonald and Wallace hopped off. The players moved seamlessly through a mostly empty garage, down a flight of stairs, and out Gate E to the chartered train, three cars long. They didn't know, but nine cases of champagne—including one of Dom Perignon—had been packed in the truck hours before with their luggage, headed up the New Jersey Turnpike ahead of them. Life on the road can be routine, monotonous. In the September of a lost season, it can be deadening. This final trip—New York, Atlanta, Miami, champagne in tow—promised something more.

When the Nationals players gathered for the final game of their penultimate home stand of the year—a 4:05 p.m. start against Atlanta—they walked through the concrete concourse, added their roller bags to Wallace's pile of luggage, then entered the clubhouse. On the whiteboard just outside the main locker room, one of many places that day's lineup is posted, McDonald had neatly printed the decorum, unchanged from the beginning of the year, always worth a reminder:

Train Trip—Jeans & Dress Shirt
Plane Trips—Slacks, Dress shirts, Dress shoes

On the floor in front of each locker sat a blue bag with the club's curly W logo on the end, unmistakably Nationals gear. Into each would go baseball gloves, spikes, flip-flops, socks, sunglasses, shorts, braces, cups, ointments, lotions— the stuff the players need at the ballpark. Getaway day, as such travel days are known in the majors, is scarcely a getaway for Wallace and his staff of four full-timers and eight seasonal workers, many of whom double as batboys.

"Controlled chaos," Wallace said.

He is fifty-five and has been in major league clubhouses for nearly four decades, ever since his mother took over laundry duties when the Washington Senators moved to his hometown of Arlington and became the Texas Rangers. Back then, at fourteen, he made $4 a day for putting out laundry, shining shoes, running errands, whatever players needed whenever they needed it. The postgame spreads consisted of chips and dip, the clubhouse had one tap for soda and another for beer, players used one pair of shoes for batting practice and another for the game, and that was it. Wallace took Gaylord Perry's Lincoln Continental to his junior prom, got Izod shirts and Italian leather zip-up boots from Jim Fregosi, babysat for Buddy Bell and Sandy Alomar—players whose sons became major leaguers. Those sons have now retired, too.

Wallace was with Bo Jackson in Kansas City, won a World Series with the Florida Marlins in 1997, endured the nomadic life of the Montreal Expos in the early part of this century—when some "home" games were in Puerto Rico—and helped the Nationals transition first to RFK Stadium, where he slept during the summer of 2005, then to Nationals Park.

And for all the differences, nothing has changed.

"It can have a tendency to become *Groundhog Day*–ish," he said. "But every day, you don't know how the game's going to end. It's not like any other nine-to-fiver."

Off to the side of the clubhouse, three chefs worked on the Nationals' pregame meal. Healthy options—a chicken and a fish, sandwiches, cereal, salad—are offered every day. In 2010, when right fielder Jayson Werth was with the Philadelphia Phillies and approaching an offseason in which he would be a free agent, he stopped during batting practice one day and asked Adam Dunn, then the Nationals' first baseman, how he was treated in Washington. Forget the money for a second. How is the organization?

"Sometimes, guys'll say, 'Ehhhhh,'" Werth said. "You don't want to hear that. But he surprised me. He said he was treated great. He said he had everything he needed, that the people were great. That makes a difference."

When Werth signed with the Nationals, he went about pushing for further improvements. The kitchen staff is one element. There is now a team nutritionist, a massage therapist, a barber, and a car washer available at least once a home stand. "If we forgot something at home," said reliever Tyler Clippard, "we can ask one of these guys to run and get it, and they will. There's nothing they won't do."

It's not free, though. Each major league club charges clubhouse dues, so each National pays $95 per home date, $60 on the road to the visiting clubhouse manager. At the end of the year, most players—most, but not all—will tip the home staff, maybe 20 percent of the dues for the year. That's roughly $12,500 per player in dues per season, pre-tip. Most believe it's well worth it.

"The reality is," Storen said, "I'm pretty terrible at life during the season. These guys take the pressure off."

When the game against the Braves began, Storen came into the clubhouse wearing leggings, his uniform pants hanging in his locker. Fellow reliever Rafael Soriano sank into a couch, the MASN broadcast on a flat-screen in front of him. The end-of-the-game relievers generally hang out in the clubhouse in the early innings, and there's traffic all the time—Werth coming in between at-bats to cool off, Anthony

Rendon trying to shake a bug that kept him out of the lineup, Ian Desmond looking for a new bat.

The voice of radio play-by-play man Charlie Slowes pumped through the clubhouse speakers while Wallace's staff packed what it could during the game. Three giant washing machines churned through the uniforms and undergarments soiled during batting practice. McDonald sat in his office, chatting with Jordan Zimmermann, who had started the game the day before and idly tossed a baseball in the air, catching it in his bare hand, tossing it again.

This is a major part of the job: establishing relationships with these guys.

"I try not to ask them baseball questions," McDonald said. "They get enough of that."

The game is McDonald's downtime, practically the only time of day when someone isn't asking for something. But as the late innings descended, and the road trip grew closer, the bustle picked up. Wallace hardly noticed as Bryce Harper slugged a ninth-inning homer off Braves closer Craig Kimbrel, but he slowed to watch Danny Espinosa's at-bat before moving into the clubhouse to wheel out a cart of equipment. At 7:06 p.m., Kimbrel recorded the final out of a 6–2 Washington loss, and the Nationals slowly lumbered up the stairs to the clubhouse, toward the road.

"Ready to get outta here?" McDonald called. Each player handed his game hat to an attendant, to put it in a heavy metal box used just for caps. No movement was wasted.

"Andrew, crush the hamper and see if it'll close," Wallace said. "Adam, check the staff room and see if there's any laundry."

In the laundry room, Taylor, one of the September call-ups unfamiliar with big league life, fiddled with a handheld steamer in hopes of smoothing out his plaid shirt. Out of nowhere arrived Ryan Wiebe, an assistant who helps McDonald with the travel and Wallace in the clubhouse. Wiebe switched the machine on and began working on the shirt.

"You got to remember: Treat people how you want to be treated," McDonald said. "Treat him as if it's your kid or your cousin or your brother. What would you do for them? It doesn't always work out that way. Everyone frustrates you at some point in time. It's hard to treat Jayson Werth like he's your son. But that's how you conduct yourself."

In February, McDonald gathered with his family in Arizona, where his parents now live, to watch the Super Bowl. His daughter Riley was about to turn one. His annual rhythms—essentially unchanged since the Montreal Expos moved to Washington—had always mirrored baseball's rhythms. But here was this little girl.

"That's the hardest part," he said. "You're away, and you come back, and she's changed. I try to turn it into a positive, like I can notice the differences because I'm not there every day. But you can't get that time back."

The Seattle Seahawks beat the Denver Broncos on February 2. On February 4, McDonald was due in Viera, Florida, to prepare for spring training. The season wouldn't start for another eight weeks. During the Super Bowl, McDonald's brother began doing the math.

"Basically," he said, "you're on call till October."

McDonald could only shrug. In a way, spring training, which seems like such a slow build for the rest of baseball, is the most hectic time of year for McDonald and Wallace. McDonald spends the months after the season preparing for the next, booking hotels, arranging charter flights, setting up apartments and hotels for players and staff during spring training. Wallace and his main assistant, Dan Wallin, use that time to take inventory, to order new equipment for the next year, to arrange the shipment of gear to Florida and back.

When players begin to trickle in, the needs come in a rush. There is no lull. "You're excited to see everybody, to see how the players look, to see what people did in the offseason," McDonald said. "And you get in a rhythm once the season starts. But to be honest, by now, I'm pretty fried."

He said this in September, eating a salmon salad at Union Market, not far from his home in the District's Brookland neighborhood. McDonald grew up outside St. Louis, went to Northern Illinois to play quarterback, moved to wide receiver, then suffered a back injury that ended his football career. He transferred to the University of Arizona, studied pre-law, and decided he preferred the pursuit of a career in pro sports over law school. So he worked in Tucson rec leagues, then for a sports radio station in Phoenix, then for the Arizona Diamondbacks in spring training before landing in the Arizona Fall League, where baseball's best prospects go each year.

Gonzalez, now the Braves' manager, managed the team to which McDonald was assigned. Carlos Tosca, now Gonzalez's bench coach in Atlanta, was the bench coach back then, too. And McDonald did whatever they asked.

"He took it real seriously," Gonzalez said. "You asked him to do something—picking up the trash, grabbing laundry, whatever—he was full tilt going after it. He'd get it done and do it happily."

McDonald so impressed Gonzalez that when the latter ended up as a coach with the Florida Marlins, he recommended his young protégé. McDonald, forty-two in September 2014, has been in baseball ever since, first as an intern in the Marlins' baseball operations department and, eventually, in 2002, as the Expos' traveling secretary. He was thirty. He now knows just about everybody in baseball, has relationships with players that date back decades. But when he came to Montreal, Omar Minaya—the general manager inserted by Major League Baseball, which owned the Expos—gave him some advice.

"No matter what happens," Minaya said, "you can't lose the trust of that clubhouse."

No one knows what goes on around the Nationals more intimately than McDonald. If a potential free agent signee comes to Washington for a physical, McDonald arranges the flight, the car service, the appointment, the hotel. If a player is sent to the minors, McDonald has the conversation about his lease situation in Washington, whether he needs a rental car in Syracuse or Harrisburg or wherever. If a player's wife and family are meeting the team on the road, McDonald books an adjacent room. When it's time to distribute meal money for the road—$95 a day—McDonald hands out the envelopes. He knows who needs a gluten-free meal on the team flight, who is obsessed with fantasy football, who arrives at the ballpark early and who stays late.

"You really have to have a lot of discretion in what you do talk about and what you don't talk about," McDonald said. He will not bring every little problem to Rizzo. "You got to put out the fires. You have to take the pressure off of him as much as you do the players."

So from his spot as gatekeeper, concierge, liaison—"Kind of like our 'slash,'" Storen said—McDonald has not only watched as the Nationals have been transformed from baseball's Island of Misfit Toys into an organization that expects to compete for a division title every season, but he has helped shape it, in tiny but tangible ways. When the club contracted with a small charter company, and that company couldn't provide a replacement plane when one broke down—forcing the Nationals to sit on the tarmac for six hours, then return home at midnight before flying the next day—McDonald convinced the club it needed better services. The Nationals now charter with United.

"If Ian Desmond gets offered $100 million [as a free agent], and we offer him $80 million, it's easy," McDonald said. "You go with the $100 million. But if he gets offered $100 million from both of us, and his wife is comfortable and his family likes it here and he knows the way he's going to be treated—to us, that could make a difference."

It is why McDonald arrives at the ballpark between ten and eleven a.m. on most game days, maybe nine hours before first pitch, an hour before the coaching staff starts to trickle in, a couple of hours before the players show up. It's why, when he got off the elevator and walked across the marble floor in the lobby of the New York Palace Hotel, his phone was to his ear.

"Bus is at ten-thirty," he said. This was Sunday, the last day of a four-game series against the Mets, the day for travel to Atlanta. One bus, with the staff and a few early-rising players, had departed for Citi Field at nine a.m. Wallace was in the lobby, working with white-gloved bellmen to check off each piece of luggage headed to an equipment truck, marking his list. He grabbed his own phone and listened.

"I told him to put a tag on it," he said. He listened some more. "I'll see if I have another one," and he turned to his own roller bag, moved aside his copy of A Game of Inches:

The Stories Behind the Innovations That Shaped Baseball, and rummaged for a tag.

"The old saying: You can lead a horse to water," he said.

At that moment, the Nationals' magic number to clinch the division was 6. The second bus departed, right on time.

B y the time United flight 1809 pulled slowly into Gate D8 at Hartsfield-Jackson Atlanta International Airport, the concourse was nearly empty. The largest screen at the Atlanta Braves All Star Grill, adjacent to the gate, had long since switched off the Braves' miserable 10–3 loss to the Texas Rangers, completing a sweep. The Nationals had quickly overcome their own issues—a plane damaged by a mobile luggage ramp at New York's LaGuardia Airport, a switch to a new Boeing 737, a flight that took off just after 6:30 p.m., about an hour late.

Two buses waited on the tarmac, and a staircase wheeled over to the plane.

"People ask how often we play, which is every day, and they hear about how much we travel, which is all the time, and they're like, 'Oh, my god. I had no idea,'" Werth said. "'You must be exhausted.' And then I'm like, 'Well, you don't know how we travel.'"

For each flight, McDonald arranges with the Transportation Security Administration to have officers and screening equipment at the ballpark, so the Nationals never have to wait in line at a terminal. The buses take them directly to the plane, so there's no interminable walk at Dulles, no train ride in Atlanta.

When the plane's door swung open, Rizzo came down the stairs first and headed left to the buses. Wallace came next, and headed right, underneath the plane to the cargo hold. A single truck awaited at the end of a conveyor belt. Here came the champagne. It was 9:05 p.m.

The Nationals, buoyed by their victory over the Mets, a celebratory flight, and the potential accomplishment ahead, all but bounced down the steps, the rookies dressed in leotards as part of baseball's annual ritual of light hazing. By 9:13, the buses took off, headed to the Ritz-Carlton Buckhead. Wallace remained under the plane, grabbing bag after bag with the United staff.

One problem: There was only one truck. "There was a mix-up," Wallace said. "Put it that way." The upshot: The truck had to travel to the team hotel with the players' luggage, unload, then return to the airport, pack up the equipment, and drive to Turner Field, where John Holland, the manager of the visiting clubhouse for the Braves, awaited with his staff of seven, which passed the time by playing football in the concourse. At 11:05 p.m., the truck backed up to the door to the clubhouse, and something approaching a sporting ballet began.

"The ones that say 'V' at the top are video," Wallace said.

The Nationals' gray road pants went into the wash immediately, as did the red alternate jerseys they wore in New York. Each equipment bag landed directly in front of each player's locker, and clubhouse attendants began meticulously unpacking them, hanging warm-up jerseys and T-shirts on hangers and belts on hooks, placing deodorant and sunglasses and socks in each locker. By 11:48 p.m., the pants were out of the dryer, ready to be distributed. Wallace and Holland began discussing a potential division-clinching celebration.

"If it comes down to Wednesday," Holland said, "I've got the Mets coming in here that night."

Wallace knew what that meant: cleaning the beer and champagne out of the carpet, making it look new and unaffected for a team long since eliminated. At 12:25 a.m., the work done, one of the Braves' clubbies left Turner Field with Wallace, ready to drop him off at the team hotel.

"Well," Wallace told Holland, "we'll hope for Tuesday."

Hope, in baseball, has little correlation to reality. But when the Nationals won that Monday night, they showed up Tuesday with the chance to clinch. Holland's staff had long since installed hooks above each locker, from which the sheets of plastic that protect the players' lockers would hang. By the sixth inning that night, the plastic was up, the champagne chilled.

"There are guys in my position who always say, 'Ah, October's the hardest time of year,'" said McDonald, who faced the prospect of booking hotels in multiple cities for stays of undetermined lengths, of scheduling charters before game times are determined. "I don't look at it that way. We go through all this other stuff to be able to play an extra month of baseball. I'll take that grind of the summer every time if I know I'm going to play in October. I've been through enough seasons where we're twenty games back."

Tuesday night, the Nationals won. There was no flight to take, no pressing matter to which to attend. As the celebration raged in the middle of the clubhouse, McDonald stood at the edge, back up against the sheets of plastic, watching the frothy mayhem. He smiled, accepted handshakes and hugs that came his way. "I never played a game," he said. And yet the players in the pile wouldn't have been there without him.

DREW STOREN

The Reliever

The skies were cloudy as a September breeze pushed summer further behind, so Drew Storen altered his routine just a hair on this Wednesday. The National League East title had been sewn up the previous week, when Storen recorded the final out against the Atlanta Braves, and with autumn around the corner, a sweatshirt and jeans replaced the normal T-shirt and shorts. He popped out the back door of his high-rise apartment building in the Rosslyn neighborhood of Arlington, Virginia, just across the Potomac River from the District of Columbia, and took the same route to the same chain restaurant where the same order placed with the same app awaited him.

The worker bees who created the lunchtime din at this particular Chipotle weren't aware that the everyman digging

into a *barbacoa quesarito*, a burrito wrapped in a cheese que-
sadilla roughly the size of a Mini Cooper, had the previous
night pitched the ninth inning for the Washington Nationals. They were oblivious to the fact that he was—by factual
demonstration, if not by label or coronation—the Nationals'
closer and that, just a week and a half later, he would be in a
position to turn his most public, kick-in-the-groin disappointment into a moment that might make it impossible for him to
walk into a Chipotle and snarf down his lunch incognito.

"This is my breakfast," he said. It was 12:20 p.m. Do the
math—arrive at the park at 2:30 p.m., record the final out at
10:00 p.m., work out after the game, bring a meal home,
watch some TED Talks on Netflix, go to bed at 3:00 a.m.—
and it makes some sense.

"It's autopilot," Storen said. "I need to treat each day
the same."

So he does, even though they can end so differently. Position players who are entrenched in the lineup need their routines because they must be prepared to perform nightly,
upward of 150 times a season, and nothing can be altered or
out of place, because steadiness in the approach can lead to
steadiness in the results. That's the belief, anyway. Starting
pitchers understand that when their turn in the rotation
comes up, the previous four days must have been spent properly, building toward that once-every-five-games glare. The
rhythms are predictable and monotonous by their nature,
and most players want to keep them right there, just so.

Relief pitchers live the most curious existence in baseball. They must be ready to perform every day even though every day breaks with no way to know whether they'll be needed. It is a mental wrestling match for nearly every one of them, whether they pitch the sixth or the ninth, whether they're entrusted with protecting a narrow lead or charged with mopping up after a starter puts the team in a huge deficit. So the struggle is daily with each one of them: How do you simultaneously stay rested and in shape? How do you simultaneously remain calm and relaxed but sharp and prepared?

"You have to figure out a way to get a routine," said Tyler Clippard, long the Nationals' eighth-inning man. "And it's not easy."

Because it can be a routine that, by the end of the night, leads to removing an unsoiled uniform, placing a sweatless cap back in the locker, and going home without needing so much as a shower. In what other job do you prepare diligently for hours with a less than 50 percent chance that you will actually work? In the 2014 regular season, Storen would be called on to pitch in 65 games. That meant he stayed idle in 97, other than those times he was, as relievers say, "dry-humped," asked to warm up but then never called into the game.

An odd existence, for sure. Yet for Storen, it's normal. So many relievers are converted (read: failed) minor league starters. Storen is not. As a freshman at Stanford, the coaching staff liked his puff-out-the-chest attitude so much that they felt he could help at the end of games, even as a nineteen-year-old. In September 2014, he was twenty-seven. He has never left that role.

"I just had that adrenaline rush because of the pressure, and I loved it," Storen said. "I go, 'This is it.' It just clicked. You just have that feeling: This is what I'm supposed to do."

Storen had that feeling when he was selected out of Stanford with the tenth pick in the 2009 draft, nine picks after the Nationals made Stephen Strasburg the top choice, securing both their rotation and their bullpen for years to come. They took Storen because of his athletic delivery, his electric fastball—and his demeanor.

"You have to have a little swagger to you to compete back there" at the end of games, Nationals general manager Mike Rizzo said. "There's nobody warming up when you're in the game. That's it. The game's over one way or the other when you're in there. The weight of the world is either lifted off your shoulders—or it's on your shoulders."

Chowing on lunch, Storen had felt the weight, had it lifted, felt the weight again. He began the season as the Nationals' seventh-inning reliever, an important but not glamorous job, and not the one he preferred. "Any role he has, he accepts," said Jay Lehr, the pitching coach who began working with Storen when he was eight, back in his native Indianapolis. "But he *loves* to close, I can tell you that. He's got it turned on every day. That's the thing that drives him."

As he sat at Chipotle and the cool of September settled in, he was the closer, receiving the credit while knowing blame constantly lurked, just around the corner. The division title was in hand. The playoffs awaited, with no way to control the challenges they would bring. So the controllables sat in front of him, a *barbacoa quesarito*, same as it ever was.

F or hitter or pitcher, rookie or veteran, baseball has long been defined by failure rather than success, the old a-.300-hitter-gets-out-7-times-in-10-at-bats truism. Dealing with and managing failure is an essential—some would say *the* essential—part of the job description.

"This game will tear you apart," said Craig Stammen, a Washington reliever and one of Storen's closest friends on the team, "and it always humbles you."

There is no way to truly understand the role of a reliever—the demands and the rhythms, the angst and the glory—without understanding failure. Here, though, was Drew Storen's path to becoming a major league closer: two years at Stanford in which he struck out 116 men in 99 innings. When he left college, he had one goal: "I just wanted to get to the big leagues as fast as I could."

Fast enough? Eleven appearances in low–Class A as a professional debut, seven more appearances at high–Class A to begin swiftly moving up the chain, 10 scoreless outings in Class AA by the end of his first summer. His first spring training, he was in big league camp. When the season opened, he blew through a stint at Class AA, then another at Class AAA. When he made his major league debut on May 17, 2010—less than a year after he was drafted—he had dominated the minors with a 1.68 ERA and 64 strikeouts in 53 and ⅔ innings. By the trade deadline that summer, the Nationals were sure enough about Storen's future that they traded away incumbent Matt Capps. By the next summer, Storen saved 43 games.

Failure? Almost none of it. The learning felt easy. Even when there was a blip—those 43 saves in 2012 were coupled with 5 blown opportunities—he knew how relievers must handle things. In football, cornerbacks who are burned deep must erase failure quickly because the next bomb is only a play away. Relievers are no different. Lose a lead? Make sure that *barbacoa quesarito* is waiting for you the next day to start all over again.

"You never want to tell how you did last night by the way you walked in," Storen said. "If I come in and I struggled the day before, I always wanted the ball the next day because I want to go out there and punch back hard. I loved that from the start. I loved the fact that I don't have to sit on it for four or five days. You learn to have short-term memory."

But the evaluation of each performance is harsher, particularly externally, because success is expected. A starter might give up three runs in the first but then make it through six innings right there, with his team in the game. If he does, he's commended. A reliever gives up three runs? It's his only inning, and he's the goat.

"It takes a toll on you a lot more than if you have a bad start because you're expected to go out there and get the job done, especially when you just have to get three outs," Clippard said. "So from that sense, it's more of a jolt to your system, more of like, 'Man, I kind of let myself down, let the team down.'"

The mission, for a reliever, is to limit the impact of the jolts. So whether he was pitching in the seventh or the ninth, Storen left for the ballpark at the same time—arriving at or about 2:30 p.m. for a 7:00 p.m. start—to approach the same routine. On this September Wednesday, the valet in his building pulled his massive pickup truck—a Ford F-150 Raptor by Roush Performance, encased in a vinyl pattern that, Storen said proudly, makes it "one of one"—and he took his same-as-every-other-day route to the ballpark, a quick jump down the George Washington Parkway along the Potomac, north on I-395, south on South Capitol Street, left on Potomac Avenue and into the players' lot, where he tries to find the same under-the-building spot each day.

There is intentional routine in all this, but feathered in is a pursuit of excellence, too. Storen clearly seeks the best of whatever's around. When he stopped to check on a package delivery at his building's front desk, he pored over the concierge's new iPhone 6, comparing it to and contrasting it with his Samsung. The living room wall of his

walk-right-off-the-elevator apartment was lined with ten put-
ters, many of them Scotty Cameron collector's editions—a
Clint Eastwood model anchored by bullet shells—one of
seventy-five ever made—a Tiger Woods Masters edition, on
and on. In his five seasons in Washington, Storen had lived
all over the city—with Clippard on Capitol Hill, in Penn
Quarter by himself, in Georgetown. In 2014, he settled into
Northern Virginia because the brief commute gives him
time to catch up with people—his parents, his fiancée back
in Indianapolis—that might otherwise go untended to.

"I can get too much in the bubble," he said. The season,
every day of it, is an obsession, and the bubble is both necessary and counterproductive. When Storen walked from his
truck to the door that led him inside Nationals Park, down a
ramp to the home clubhouse, he stopped along the security
fence to sign autographs for the hounds that are out there
daily, five or six hours before a game. "Congratulations," they
said, thrusting hands and photos and Sharpies through the
metal bars, and Storen thanked them back. This was a high
point. The game the night before marked his eighteenth
straight appearance without allowing a run. His last six
appearances had all resulted in saves. His ERA for the season
was down to a teensy-weensy 1.23. It never, even for a day,
was above 2.00 all year. He would close in the playoffs.

"He's becoming more of a veteran pitcher now," Rizzo
said. "He knows better how to prepare this year. He's a guy
you have to tell to back off, not to hurry up."

His ability to back off has evolved during his time in the majors. His first professional spring training he was so excited, bouncing from place to place and drill to drill, even from his locker to the shower, that he lost fifteen pounds. Using that kind of energy, he discovered, isn't sustainable. So by 2014, his rhythms were locked in. At the park a good seven hours before he's likely to pitch, he lifted light weights, swam a little bit, warmed up his shoulder with elastic bands, then headed out to the field to throw from flat ground in the outfield. He and the other relievers stretch their warm-up tosses out to 120 or 150 feet, then come closer, in to 60 feet, and they toss versions of their pitches to one another. Even now, Storen likes to throw a little longer and a little harder than his peers do, so a catcher eventually replaces his partner, and he works more on his stuff. This pregame work all built to each day's most important development: foosball with Clippard. They got so into it that they bought a table off Craigslist and stuck it down in a small alcove by the batting cages, just down a short hall from the home dugout, and as the fans filtered in about 5:45 p.m., the two relief pitchers engaged in testy matches.

"We want to compete at everything we do—who's got the cool golf clubs, the best shot, who putts better, who's the best foosball player," Clippard said.

There are, too, serious games of golf. Clippard is an excellent player, a 4 handicap, and Stammen has been playing his whole life as well. Storen took up the game more seriously only in the previous two years, and he gets furious when he struggles by comparison. But they all lug their golf bags on the road, all make early-morning tee times even on some days when they play, because it can actually serve as preparation. It gets their bodies moving.

"It teaches you about being a reliever," Storen said. "You double [bogey] a hole, and you say, 'I need to birdie the next two.' Well, what are you going to do? You're going to try to kill it, and it's going to be a disaster. I think golf is as parallel as you're going to get to being a reliever."

So the preparation toggles between goofy and serious, golf and foosball and DVDs alternating with somber assessments of their bodies, which must be tended to constantly. Storen, over time, has learned everything he could about the kinetic chain, about how a bad left hip can lead to a right shoulder injury. Every couple of weeks during the season, he brings out his hometown masseuse—with whom he has worked since he was a teenager—to get his aches and pains flushed out. When his masseuse isn't around, he is obsessive about "foam rolling," essentially giving himself a massage by rolling a piece of PVC pipe covered in black foam, and even a little rope for texture, all over his body.

"It's a Band-Aid," he said, and not a day goes by when he's not working on some part of his body. He might do it even when the game begins. Storen and Clippard and the other late-inning relievers remain in the clubhouse even after first pitch, soaking in a cool tub, then a hot tub, then back in the cool tub to further prepare their muscles. As they get fully dressed, they watch the televisions near their lockers, taking in the strike zone for the night, glancing at hitters' tendencies. Storen usually gets to the bullpen by the fourth inning.

That didn't change, whether he was due to pitch the seventh, as he did in May, or the ninth, as he did in September.

"Before, I was pumped," he said. "I wanted to be the closer. Everybody in the bullpen wants to be the closer. Who doesn't want to be? That's natural competitive nature.

"But if you go into it and say, 'I'm the closer,' and you have this persona, you have this whole thing you need to do, you're not concentrating on the right things. It's not like I get a 'C' patch sewn on my chest. You're a reliever. You have to get three outs. That's it."

When you do, the grind of being a closer is immensely satisfying because you're the guy shaking hands with the catcher and leading the team through the high-five line, a nightly celebration. When you don't? Well, then there is perhaps the most open wound in all of baseball, the guy left to shuffle off the field because the last out was his to get and he couldn't get it.

October baseball is littered with relievers who have been handed a lead, asked to get three outs, and been unable to do so. Donnie Moore in the 1986 American

League Championship Series. Mitch Williams in the 1993 World Series. Jose Mesa in the 1997 World Series. Shoot, Mariano Rivera, the greatest reliever ever to live, in the 2001 World Series. At some point, they were all exposed in public, on the greatest stage, unable for one night to complete their jobs.

For a hitter, the drip-drip-drip of a slump isn't visible in one moment, one at-bat, even one 0-for-4 night. To understand it involves taking a step back. But the reliever's collapse is right there, contained in a single inning or a single at-bat. And so, as Drew Storen headed into his second October as the Nationals' closer, he was buoyed by the way he pitched in 2014 with full knowledge—deep, scarring knowledge—of the kind of pain a reliever can suffer.

When the Nationals reached the postseason for the first time in franchise history, in 2012, Storen saved Game 1 of the National League Division Series against St. Louis. He pitched a scoreless inning in a loss in Game 3, then earned the win in Game 4 when Jayson Werth hit a walk-off homer to force a fifth and deciding game. At that point, he had no postseason problems: three innings pitched, no hits and no runs (and just one walk) allowed.

What happened the next night is the kind of event, for a baseball town, that makes winter feel longer and colder, the next summer, the next chance, so far off. The Nationals held a 7–5 lead in the ninth, a sellout crowd stood in anticipation, and Storen had the ball. In his past 19 outings, he had allowed one run. The Cardinals got a double and then moved that runner to third, but Storen also got two outs. He then nearly had Yadier Molina struck out, but a close two-strike pitch was called a ball, and Molina walked. He nearly had David Freese struck out, but another two-strike pitch was called a ball, and Freese walked, too. And then there was the little ground ball back up the middle by a St. Louis utility man named Daniel Descalso that tied the game, then the two-run single from a shortstop named Pete Kozma that won it for the Cardinals, that ended the Nationals' season.

"He was at the top of his baseball career," said Stammen, who joined Clippard as one of Storen's closest friends on the Nationals. "He was the closer on the team that had the most wins in Major League Baseball that year. . . . And he had one bad game, and that pretty much ruined his baseball life for about a year."

The open wound the Cardinals inflicted that night festered into the offseason, even as Storen knew he was comfortable with the pitches he threw and the times he threw them. But his 2013 season was a perfect example of how one poor outcome can affect the next, the exact opposite of what a reliever wants to do. In the offseason, the Nationals signed Soriano, a veteran who had closed with the Rays and the Yankees. Storen's response seemed defiant, not against the club or against Soriano. But he badly wanted to show that one unfortunate inning hadn't destroyed him.

"I probably tried to do too much," Storen said. "I didn't

want to give up a run all year. It wasn't showing somebody. It's showing the game. It's the baseball gods, right?"

So to appease the gods, he changed things, which would only serve to roil them. His entry music at Nationals Park had always been "Bad Company," a growling, in-your-face cover of a '70s song by the band Five Finger Death Punch. He switched to the more subdued "When the Lights Go Out" by the Black Keys. By late July, his delivery was a mess, his ERA nearly 6.00. Rizzo called him in for the necessary discussion: You have to go to the minor leagues.

"All athletes go through those times of turmoil, those times where you're not performing at the level that you know you're capable of," Clippard said. "But those times are as important as the times that you're doing well, because you learn the most about yourself when the cards are against you, when you're down.

"But most of the time, those times happen in the minor leagues. Drew got to the big leagues really fast. Everyone saw that struggle [in 2013] in the big leagues. It was in the public eye. That's different. That's harder."

At Class AAA Syracuse, the eye is less public, but the struggles are real. Storen made six appearances there, trying to get back his delivery, trying to do a better job of holding on runners, addressing exactly who was responsible for his fate: himself.

"My goal was to get back as quick as possible," Storen

said. "How do you do that? Fix it. I knew that it's easy to fall into that trap of, 'I shouldn't be here.'"

Thinking back on that time, barely a year removed from it, he started wrapping up what was left of his *quesarito*. "I never finish it," he said. He walked back to his apartment, had the truck brought around, and drove to the ballpark with no idea whether he would pitch that night or the next or the next.

"Someone said to me, 'Your warm-up song is boring,'" he said. "That's what I want: boring."

Because for a reliever, boring means routine, even when there isn't one to find. Storen would pitch in just two more games before the playoffs. And then, on October 4, the Nationals led the San Francisco Giants 1–0 in the ninth inning of Game 2 of their division series. Right-hander Jordan Zimmermann, brilliant all evening, allowed a two-out walk. And here came Storen to close it out. It just can't be boring all the time.

MIKE RIZZO

The
General Manager

Most of the lights were dark on United 1809, non-stop overnight from San Francisco to Dulles, the final charter of the year. The season was over, left in the mess of the fourth game of the National League Division Series, won by the San Francisco Giants. There is no uniform way to process such a fate, when the relentlessness of 162 games crashes into a space that, by comparison, feels tightly confined, like crawling from an open pasture into a cramped, airtight box, no room to breathe.

"You're trying to digest over two hundred days of baseball," said Ian Desmond, the Nationals' shortstop. "It's just . . . I don't know. It's so much to think about."

So the plane was mostly silent, mostly dark, completely

somber. In the first row, one light shone over one open tray table, papers pulled from a folder and spread about. This was in the wee hours of October 8, 2014. Yet the papers in front of Mike Rizzo had on them the Nationals' forty-man roster for 2015, what the payroll might be in 2017, depth charts for the future. Not a single item pertained to the bitterness that hovered throughout the cabin.

"This is my therapy," Rizzo said later. On that flight, in Rizzo's mental calculation, "this year" changed from 2014 to 2015.

Rizzo's title with the Nationals is President of Baseball Operations and General Manager, but he is one of thirty men in baseball known to the fan base as a GM. Every player who took the field in a Nationals uniform during the regular season and the playoffs, every player who took that flight back, did so because, to varying degrees, Rizzo wanted him there. His job, at its core, is to build a roster of players who complement one another in the lineup and on the pitching staff, and then hand that roster to the field manager to do with what he sees fit in each of 162 games.

But that is a simplistic analysis, and those sheets in front of Rizzo on the folding tray table in front of him would show it. The modern general manager oversees an organization of two hundred players, dozens of scouts and a front office of more than forty people that is responsible for player acquisition and development, statistical analysis—what Rizzo has come to call a "global" view. He must understand how to acquire players through the amateur draft, which covers the United States and Puerto Rico; from Latin America, where players can sign as free agents when they're sixteen years old; from Asia, where Japanese and Korean professional teams can demand a fee for a player they decide to sell to the majors; through free agency, in which relationships with agents and knowledge of the market are essential; and through trades, in which the back-and-forth with other general managers might last weeks, but which Rizzo loves.

"In that position, you've got to be playing three-dimensional chess," said Stan Kasten, the president of the Los Angeles Dodgers who held the same position with the Nationals from 2006 through 2010 and hired Rizzo first as a scouting director, then as general manager. "You've got to be thinking about this year. I think all of us agree this year's the most important. But you can't lose sight of the future. How do you balance that?"

Rizzo is bald, fit, likes a rich cigar and a light beer. He grew up on Chicago's Waveland Avenue, the same street that runs behind the left-field wall at Wrigley Field, home to the Cubs. His father, Phil, drove a truck for the city, scouted baseball on the side, and imbued in his four children a toughness worthy of the City of Broad Shoulders. Mike, the second youngest, carries it to this day. He used to take 250 ground balls every Sunday, smacked by Phil or one of his brothers. In 1982, 553 players were taken ahead of him in the draft, but that he was taken at all was a testament not to his talent but to what scouts call "makeup," the way a player comports himself and competes. Even to this day, if the situation calls for a verbal brawl, Rizzo doesn't mind throwing the first punch. When Philadelphia ace Cole Hamels admitted, in 2012, that he had intentionally hit Nationals outfielder Bryce Harper, then a rookie, with a pitch, Rizzo came out firing to *The Washington Post*. "I've never seen a more classless, gutless, chickenshit act in my thirty years in baseball," he said publicly. To those who have heard him in private, it hardly amounts to a surprise.

During those days on Waveland Avenue, it was nearly impossible to envision Mike Rizzo as an executive overseeing all the baseball elements for a business *Forbes* valued at $700 million. After attending Saint Xavier University on Chicago's South Side, he played as an infielder in the Angels' system for three seasons before being released. This would be the point when most people, just told they were washed up as players, might return home and look for a "real" job. But what Rizzo learned during those days in Class A, playing in Peoria, Illinois, in the evening, then heading to the bar to talk about the game as night turned to morning, then waking up late the next day to listen to the Cubs' pregame on the radio before heading to the ballpark again, was that he loved the life. He didn't want to leave it. He *couldn't* leave it.

"Shit," Rizzo said, almost thirty years after he faced the decision. "What else was I gonna do? I loved waking up and thinking about baseball. I loved talking about it after the game. I loved watching guys, studying them."

So after a year as a graduate assistant coach at the University of Illinois, he signed on as a scout with the Chicago White Sox. General managers these days are more likely to come from Yale or Harvard than they are from the back roads of the scouting world. Headed into the 2015 season, six GMs came from Ivy League schools, another went to MIT, another to Stanford, three more to prestigious Amherst College. Yet Rizzo's education, to him, was more practical. For a dozen years, he drove hundreds of miles at a time, packing his car for a month. It is a loner's life, a life that informs the way Rizzo conducts himself in his current job.

"Mike trusts, really, one person the most, and that's Mike," said Harolyn Cardozo, Rizzo's executive assistant since he took the general manager's role with the Nationals in 2009. "And I wonder if it weren't for the onset of sabermetrics, could he do this whole job himself, without anyone? I wonder."

It is worth wondering, because where some people get worn down by the grind, Rizzo embraces it. "Just so much energy," said Kris Kline, an old minor league teammate in Peoria, long a baseball brother.

So to those who know him, it made sense that Rizzo's light remained on aboard United 1809. Three days earlier, when the team headed to San Francisco, it had just lost a record-setting, marathon, 6-hour, 23-minute, 18-inning game to fall two games behind the Giants, a game in which pitcher Jordan Zimmermann had retired 20 straight men and held a 1–0 lead with 2 outs in the ninth. Zimmermann then issued a walk, and manager Matt Williams replaced him with Drew Storen, the closer. The next two Giants managed hits to tie the game, and a full nine innings later, rookie Tanner Roark allowed the home run that gave San Francisco an epic win, not to mention a massive advantage in the best-of-five series.

Rizzo's job on that flight was to buck up whomever he could. With the plane quiet, he walked to the back, to the players. He made sure to touch base with both Storen and Roark. "They gave something up," Rizzo said, "so you've got to be attentive to them. You've got to let them know that you still trust 'em." He had to prop up Williams, in his first year as a manager, as he wrestled with the decision that paralyzed Washington: Should he have replaced Zimmermann with Storen?

"He was hurting," Rizzo said.

The flight back from San Francisco, though, coupled that pain with unmistakable finality. Rizzo had a meaningful exchange with Adam LaRoche, the team's first baseman for the previous four seasons. The Nationals had an option on LaRoche's contract they could pick up for the 2015 season, and though it was unsaid in those hours after the loss, both men knew the club would move on. Rizzo thanked

LaRoche not just for the 82 homers he hit in a Washington uniform, but for his professionalism, his presence in the clubhouse, his service.

"It's like you're never going to see each other again," Rizzo said.

When they landed at Dulles around eight a.m. and bused to Nationals Park to pick up their cars and scatter into winter, Washington glowed in a brilliant fall day. Rizzo went home to his condo downtown to try to get some sleep but couldn't, so he threw on a pair of sneakers and came back to the ballpark, to his second-floor office with its windows along South Capitol Street across from a U-Haul franchise, its view northwest to the Washington Monument. He is fidgety by nature. Standing, holding an everyday conversation, it's as if he's in the batter's box, adjusting his sleeves and his belt and his collar. With the offseason abruptly upon him, he couldn't slow down.

"My mind was moving," he said. "My mind was racing."

There are two whiteboards in his office, one that holds magnets bearing the names of each player at each level of the Nationals' system, from rookie ball to the majors, broken down by position, and another closer to his desk on which Rizzo can scribble thoughts. For seventy-two hours, he found himself in something of a focused fog. He didn't sleep, his mind on the 2015 team. LaRoche would be gone. Reliever Rafael Soriano would be gone. Five key players—Desmond, Zimmermann, pitcher Doug Fister, center fielder Denard

Span, and reliever Tyler Clippard—were all due to be free agents after the following season. Rizzo had drafted Zimmermann when he was the Nats' scouting director, traded for both Fister and Span, helped turn Clippard from a starter into one of the best setup men in the game, resisted pressure from others in the organization who thought Desmond should have been traded following the 2011 season.

"I'm very close to the players," Rizzo said. "They know I've got their back. I've never said a bad word about a player in my life to the media. Now, we've had some screaming matches with each other many times. But they know at the end of the day I've got their back.

"But I can't fall in love with 'em. I don't love 'em. I can't."

So on those sheets on the airplane, on the whiteboard in his office, they are names and pieces, all with skill sets and contract statuses and dollar figures attached to them, figures in this game of three-dimensional chess. It was still October 2014, the players' season just over. Rizzo's season, in a way, had just started. He had to think about not just the next spring and summer, but the spring and summer after that. As constructed, with no additions, the Nationals would likely be favored to return to the postseason in 2015—and then could lose all those free agents the following winter. Would Rizzo be willing to trade one or more of those players, breaking up a group that had won two division titles in three years, sacrificing the present for the future?

"Shit, those are the questions you ask yourself every day,"

Rizzo said. "What are you risking? You're taking something away from a 96-win team. Can you really do that?"

There are times, though, when it is clear, when a general manager must act. On the night of July 22, the Nationals played the second of three games in Colorado, the first stop on a three-city trip that would carry them right up to the end of July, right to the brink of the trade deadline. More than any general manager in the game, Rizzo is with his team, on the field for batting practice prior to games, in and out of the clubhouse and the coaches' office, talking with Williams three or four times a day, breaking down a game or a decision, a player's surge or his slump. With rare exception, he makes every road trip.

"This is the group I put together," Rizzo said. "I think it tells the players that I'm accessible, that I'm there. If Ian Desmond has a problem, he knows he doesn't have to look for me. He's going to run into me."

"It's a little bit different than a lot of places where the GM doesn't come in the clubhouse, but it's not that he's there to pass judgment or to make a judgment about anything," Williams said. "He's there to simply say, 'What do we need?' . . . He loves the process."

In Colorado, Rizzo stared not only at his team but at the week ahead—annually among the busiest in the sport, with contending teams in pursuit of the final piece that might make them a champion, with also-rans making harsh self-assessments that they better play for the future, peddling away their players. In the summer of 2014, two of the best pitchers in the game—Jon Lester and David Price—were traded on July 31, with Oakland general manager Billy Beane making the first all-in move to land Lester, and Dave Dombrowski, Beane's counterpart in Detroit, punching back and snaring Price. Rarely do general managers work harder in a more condensed and pressurized environment than in the final weeks of July.

But at that point, what did the Nationals need? Nothing, really. When they faced the Rockies, they led the National League East by a game and a half over Atlanta. Moreover, they finally had their full lineup together. Ryan Zimmerman and Bryce Harper were both back from thumb injuries. Fister hadn't missed a start since opening the season on the disabled list, and lefty Gio Gonzalez was healthy again after missing a month. They had won 13 of their past 18 games, their best baseball of the year. They were trending upward.

But in the top of the sixth inning that night, Ryan Zimmerman sprinted down the first-base line, trying to beat out a double-play ball. When he did, he tumbled to the turf, called out, and grimaced in pain. He had to be helped from the field, all but dragging his right leg. "I knew right then it was two or three weeks," said Rizzo. The MRI the next morning presented the worst-case scenario: a torn hamstring in Zimmerman's right leg. "I knew then that he was out for the season."

The Nationals, wary of allowing that info to be a competitive advantage, didn't announce their internal assessment. But Rizzo clearly had a crisis. Zimmerman was scorching, hitting .387 over the previous 17 games. For Williams, Zimmerman's injury meant machinations in his lineup, juggling pieces and parts. He would move Anthony Rendon from second base back to third, where he had played when Zimmerman was out with his earlier thumb injury, and put Danny Espinosa at second. Even with the switch-hitting Espinosa sputtering badly as a hitter, it was a simple solution, a tourniquet that might get them through the rest of the season.

Almost immediately, though, Rizzo's job became far more complex.

"Several things came into my mind," Rizzo said. "Espi was struggling mightily hitting left-handed. He was okay right-handed, but we were putting [utility man Kevin] Frandsen out there at times. We were piecing it together day by day.

"So I knew at that time that I needed to make a move—if not so much for that one player at second base, then for the other twenty-four guys. I thought that the team needed to see me do my job to help them to get to where we wanted to go."

Rizzo and his top lieutenants—assistant general manager Bryan Minniti, director of baseball operations Adam Cromie, vice president of development Doug Harris, and director of player development Mark Scialabba among them—began tossing around names, potential solutions. What about Daniel Murphy of the New York Mets? Arizona had a veteran in Aaron Hill and a youngster in Didi Gregorius. And if the Diamondbacks were willing to deal, how about Martin Prado—a better hitter than the other two—to play third base, keeping Rendon at second?

Internally, the research on all these players—and others—began. The members of Rizzo's analytics team looked at all the potential candidates, trying to forecast what each might give the Nationals over the final two months of the regular season and, they hoped, deep into October. Scouts filed reports. No one, internally or externally, knew whether the Nationals would actually acquire any of these players. But for every trade that is ultimately executed, maybe twenty die without seeing light. Each set of discussions has its own flow, its own life, whether it works out or not.

Some can be contentious and drawn-out. The previous winter, coming off a disappointing second-place finish, the Nationals had two primary areas for improvement: the starting rotation and the bench. Internally, they talked about several potential pitchers, starting with a trio from the Detroit Tigers—Max Scherzer, Rick Porcello, and Fister—but including a wide array of targets, from Dillon Gee of the Mets to Jorge de la Rosa of the Rockies. When they eventually focused on Fister, the deal took shape over the weeks around

Thanksgiving. It is the guts of what a general manager does, often in secret, with only his top aides knowing the details of the discussions.

The Tigers wanted to include reliever Phil Coke and make it a four-for-two swap in which they would have received pitching prospects Robbie Ray, Taylor Jordan, and Ian Krol along with utility man Steve Lombardozzi. The Nationals didn't want Coke and his 5.40 ERA, and Rizzo didn't feel like he could part with both Ray and Jordan, a pair of promising young starters. When they finally settled on a three-for-one trade—Ray, Krol, and Lombardozzi for Fister—the Lerner family, which owns the Nationals, killed the deal, wary of parting with Ray.

This is the kind of scenario that led Kasten to say privately to his old Nationals colleagues: "Until Mike threatens to quit, nothing happens." Rizzo is nothing if not confident in his own evaluations. But Theodore Lerner, the Nationals' managing principal owner, made himself into a real estate tycoon because he possesses inordinate patience. In business, it meant he could sit on a property in a developing neighborhood and wait years for its value to increase, stressing the importance of the next decade rather than the next day. In baseball, that meant he was attracted to young prospects like Ray who were cheap and could develop into true assets over time.

Rizzo loves prospects, too. But in his world, part of the reason to have them is to trade them away for pieces that can help immediately. With a mature roster that had already tasted winning, Rizzo wanted to jump. He was incensed that a pitcher who hadn't yet reached even Class AAA was holding up the deal.

"I tell Mike all the time, 'You're the only one here who can do anything you want,'" said Cardozo, Rizzo's longtime special assistant. "'You can do anything you want, so don't tell me you can't do it.' Because he's really the only indispensable person who works for the team."

Still, Rizzo had called the Tigers' Dombrowski to tell him he couldn't do the deal. But he did something else, too: He threatened to quit. Ownership eventually relented. The deal was back on. Ray, Krol, and Lombardozzi went to Detroit, and Fister became a National.

But in July, with the Braves breathing heavily on them from behind, there was no time for "eventually." They didn't have two weeks. Rizzo stayed with the team through the rest of the series in Colorado, then moved on to Cincinnati, and finally to Miami. Along the way, he looked at video of all manner of players, each a solution to a different degree, each with a cost. And each potential trade partner knew the Nationals needed someone in Zimmerman's absence, even if they didn't know Washington's internal assessment: Their longest-tenured player wouldn't appear again in 2014.

"The price of poker goes up because that's the way the game is: supply and demand," Rizzo said. "And we had a great demand for it. We're a team poised to win. So teams aren't just going to give you players."

By the time the Nationals reached Miami, Rizzo had focused on a potential solution. The Cleveland Indians were still on the fringes of the playoff race, but their incumbent shortstop, Asdrubal Cabrera, had a contract that ended after the season. Rizzo brought the idea to his own people of trading for Cabrera and moving him to second base. Their response amounted to a long list of reasons *not* to make the move: His offensive numbers were down. He had $3.5 million remaining on his contract, and ownership didn't want Washington to add payroll in any midseason move. He hadn't played second base since 2009.

"As the sabermetrics was saying no, in my mind, he's getting more attractive to me," Rizzo said. "I'm thinking to myself, 'Hey, Mike. That's a pretty good idea.'"

Time, though, was short, and Rizzo had to make sure Cabrera was the man he wanted. With the Nationals facing the Marlins, he brought his laptop to the visiting general manager's suite during the games at Marlins Park. He watched clips of Cabrera endlessly, muttering his thoughts to himself. "Mike will tell you that there are no statistics that will show you what he can see," Cardozo said, and if he couldn't see in person, he would evaluate on tape. By the end of these marathon sessions, Rizzo knew Cabrera's gait, his foot speed, how his body worked, how he got his bat to the ball, what his eyes did at the plate, his arm strength, his dexterity. He was sitting at a major league game overseeing a major league team, and he was a scout again.

"He started out as an evaluator, so he knows what he's looking at," said Kris Kline, Rizzo's old minor league teammate who was by then his scouting director. "And since then, he's just kind of come full circle and developed into this guy that's absolutely fearless when it comes to making baseball decisions."

When Rizzo was comfortable with what he saw out of Cabrera, he reached out to Cleveland general manager Chris Antonetti, who was willing to trade Cabrera. In return, he wanted a prospect—one out of a group of pitchers A. J. Cole and Blake Treinen and outfielders Steven Souza Jr. and Michael Taylor, the same four players almost all teams inquired about when doing business with the Nationals. Rizzo would not part with any of them for a two-month rental, so the Indians asked about lower-level prospects, shortstop Wilmer Difo and outfielder Rafael Bautista, teammates in Class A.

Rizzo couldn't pull the trigger on any of those players, some of the most promising in the Nationals' system. "If I couldn't make a deal," he said, "I'd be disappointed, and I'd be disappointed for the guys. But it had to make sense. I can't just do one to do one."

After they blew a ninth-inning lead in the first game in Miami, the Nationals sleepwalked through a 3–0 loss the next night, managing five hits. Zimmerman's injury was having an impact on both the lineup and the team's psyche. Rizzo kept talking to Antonetti, and another name came up:

twenty-four-year-old infielder Zach Walters, called up from Class AAA Syracuse to be a role player when Zimmerman went down.

When Cleveland agreed to pay the remaining money on Cabrera's contract, Rizzo decided he could part with Walters. In the hours before the four p.m. July 31 deadline, the Nationals traded Walters for Cabrera, and immediately clenched their teeth and headed to the final two months of the season. The general manager's job was done, but there remained a pennant to win.

The beer bottles stacked up at the corner of the bar, Miller Lites and Amstel Lights mostly, where Mike Rizzo had set up shop for the time being. It was past eleven p.m. on a December night at Redfield's Sports Bar, tucked at the north end of the lobby of the Manchester Grand Hyatt, right on San Diego Bay. Nearly every essential decision maker from every major league team would make his way through the hotel over the course of four nights during the second week of December for baseball's annual Winter Meetings, part trade show, part conference, part media circus, highlighted by myriad top-secret rendezvous. Sit in the marble-floored lobby during the day, and almost anyone might walk by—Yankees general manager Brian Cashman, World Series heroes Curt Schilling and Jack Morris, former players who are now scouts, former players who are now announcers, legendary reporter Peter Gammons, outgoing commissioner Bud Selig, college kids decked out in coats and ties quick with a handshake and an introduction, hoping to break into the game at any level, each one of them a GM in waiting.

Over the years, the Winter Meetings have morphed from what was an essential time to get together and swap ideas and players to an around-the-clock rumor-fest fueled by reporters, agents, scouts, social media, and executives—not necessarily in that order. At a time on the calendar when baseball would otherwise seem dead, the meetings attract attention to the sport. The very night that Rizzo sat at Redfield's, mingling with several members of his front office and scouting staff while a group of Yankees personnel surrounded an adjacent table, the televisions above the bar and on the walls showed the news on the ticker: The Chicago Cubs had agreed to terms on a six-year, $155 million deal with free agent lefty Jon Lester.

Some people in baseball believe that, with e-mail and virtual conferencing and document sharing and all the conveniences of modern life, the Winter Meetings have passed their time. Rizzo disagrees. "I love 'em," Rizzo said, and he knew exactly how the week would go, ending with him collapsing into an airplane seat, sleeping the entire flight home.

The meetings technically run from a Monday morning through Thursday around noon, but the baseball world begins gathering on the Sunday night prior, and that's when

Rizzo arrived in San Diego. The offseason had started on that flight back from San Francisco, and it hadn't stopped. The early weeks are filled with procedural decisions, the equivalent of a player taking his first few cuts in the cage at spring training: whom to keep on the forty-man roster and therefore protect from other teams, which contract options to exercise to keep a player around, which departing free agents to offer contracts to—because doing so brings a draft pick as compensation should they sign with another team.

Every year, be it following 90 wins or 90 losses, there must be a postmortem, both with the front office staff and with the manager, in this case Williams, whom Rizzo hired following the 2013 season. So after Williams had a few days to decompress at his home in the Washington suburb of Chevy Chase, Maryland, he came in and sat in a leather chair in Rizzo's office. This was informal but important. The swirl around Williams, in the wake of the loss to the Giants, had been brutal. Fans and analysts had questioned pulling Zimmermann in Game 2. Worse, people had ridiculed his handling of the bullpen in the fourth game, when the Giants clinched. He left rookie Aaron Barrett in, never used a rested Strasburg as a reliever, on and on.

"He took it extremely hard," Rizzo said. "I showed my support in all the decisions he made. But I think the postseason was weighing on him."

The two men talked for hours. This part of the year, for a manager, is supposed to be for recouping and relaxing. But

Williams had to shake off the postseason. Rizzo—who hired him and therefore is more invested in his success than anyone in the organization—had to help him.

"We both understand, everybody understands, that one play or one pitch or whatever—it can make or break you," Williams said. "I think if I know him, he immediately switches focus to, 'Okay, what do we need to do next time? What do we need to do for the next season to get back to that point?' And he helped me do that."

In the course of these end-of-season interviews and front office discussions, needs are identified. The Nationals, clearly, needed a second baseman for 2015, preferably a left-handed hitter, even more preferably someone who could move to shortstop the following year should the team not re-sign Desmond. And while deals can and do happen at any time, there is a rhythm to the offseason, just as there is to the spring-training-to-Opening-Day-to-All-Star-break-to-dog-days-to-pennant-races regular season. On a given day in his office—adorned with mementos that tie him back home: a Chicago Bears helmet, a Waveland Avenue street sign, a Bobby Hull Blackhawks sweater mingling with the items from his time as the Nationals' general manager—Rizzo will put out and take two dozen phone calls, agents and executives from other teams, his own staff, and his dad, who's an adviser still.

This builds to the general managers' meetings, held in November 2014 at the posh Arizona Biltmore Hotel in

Phoenix. Rizzo heads to each of these affairs with a sheet on each team identifying potential trade targets. He touched base with every franchise, each of which knew his situation with Desmond, Zimmermann, and the other players in the last year of their contracts. "I'm ready to deal right then," he said. "You want to make a deal? Let's go. If you want to get specific, I'll get specific. We've got all-stars we would move in the right deal." But in Phoenix, he found no matches. He and his staff regrouped, headed home, and brought their business to San Diego a month later.

There, in a suite on the eighth floor of the Manchester Grand's Seaport Tower, Rizzo gathered his entire staff of executives, analysts, and scouts each morning of the Winter Meetings. His own room was adjacent, and it is there he would retire to take the most important calls, those from other general managers should a deal be getting close. But in the mornings he would infuse his staff with energy, surrounding a large table in the center of the room, laptops open and buzzing, as they considered all options to improve. Potential trade scenarios were written on a whiteboard. Rizzo took notes on them all, and asked certain groups to break off to talk about and pick apart players.

"This scenario is perfect for him," Williams said one morning, standing in the hall outside the suite. "It's completely his sweet spot because he gets to talk to all the scouts. They talk the same language."

The Nationals had several potentially moving parts. They

could deal Clippard, perhaps at the height of his value. They could shake up the sport and trade Desmond or Zimmermann. Left-hander Ross Detwiler, a former first-round pick, also had only one year remaining on his contract, there was no place for him in the rotation, and he hadn't been particularly effective as a reliever. For years, Rizzo would be at these meetings offering his opinions to his general manager about players he had scouted, players that might be trade targets. Now he would ask his staff: What do you think of this guy? And he'd have to trust them.

"It was the toughest thing I had to learn," Rizzo said. "When I have an opinion, when I've seen a guy and can rely on my evaluation instincts, I'm good with making that decision. The toughest part is to make decisions, make trades, make major trades, do major acquisitions on players that you haven't really seen recently or at all, and you're trusting your evaluators to give you the road map on what decision to make."

By design, though, the men in that room on the eighth floor of the Seaport Tower had been in the game for decades. When Rizzo first became a scout, his policy was to get to the ballpark early, not say a word, and listen to the veterans. Now the scouts in that room were the types of guys he used to listen to—confident in what they see, what they know, not a yes-man among them.

"There is no bullshit," Rizzo said. "Scouting is opinions. Who knows? That bullshit opinion, maybe it turns out to be right. We never find out who's right or who's wrong for years.

"Everybody's opinion counts, but that doesn't mean that we're not going to dissect the shit out of it and hammer the shit out of it. There's certain times that I'm gonna test you. You're gonna say that 'this guy's no good.' Well, why is he no good? When I put the heat on somebody, if they back off it, then that says something about their conviction on 'that player."

There is no end to the conversations, not during the meetings, not all year. That night, Rizzo sat at the bar and swapped old minor league stories with Kline: the time Kline threw his bat in anger after a pop-up; the bar they used to close in Peoria; their old manager Joe Maddon, who had risen to lead the Tampa Bay Rays to the World Series before becoming one of the lead story lines of the 2014–15 offseason when he moved on to the Chicago Cubs. Rizzo reveled in telling them all, then leaned against the wall to listen to Kasey McKeon, who serves as the Nationals director of player procurement. Jimmy Gonzales, Jeff Zona, Fred Costello— all his scouts, all his guys—chatted as midnight passed. The topic did not waver: baseball. Present or past, but always baseball.

At one a.m., the lights came up and the bar closed. Rizzo walked into the lobby. The elevator awaited, followed not long after by the next morning's meeting and the rest of the offseason—*his* season, because he still had a team to improve.

The Winter

Ryan Zimmerman drove through the suburbs of Northern Virginia, more maintenance necessary on a January morning. His daughter Mackenzie, not yet fourteen months old, had just completed her second Christmas, bouncing from her grandparents' house in Ryan's hometown of Virginia Beach to her great-grandfather's house in the sand hills of North Carolina to his in-laws' home in the Washington suburbs, ripping open whatever present was placed before her, delighting in—if not understanding—it all.

Each of these January drives marked a contrast for Zimmerman, monotony paired with excitement. The offseason offers time for reflection, but only if you allow yourself to reflect. This was Zimmerman's second January as a father, but his first as a thirty-year-old, his first as a first baseman. Behind him were 1,198 major league games. With him was a ragged shoulder and a healed hamstring. Ahead of him was the chiropractor and what that represented, his new reality.

"Everybody laughs at me when I say I'm old," Zimmerman said. But in this shoulder season, he felt just that. Chiropractors aren't for twenty-year-olds. Third basemen become first basemen only if they can no longer perform their previous jobs.

At some point each winter for every single person involved in baseball, "this season" becomes "last season" and "next season" becomes "this season." The pivot point varies for each, owing to some combination of personal proclivities and life events. By January, though, Zimmerman needed to think not about the wrecked season behind him, when a broken thumb and a torn hamstring limited him to 61 games, fewer than in any of his nine full seasons in the majors, and kept him on the bench at the most important time of year, the playoffs. He needed to think about the spring that lay ahead, when he would officially end the charade he had been forced to perpetrate for more than two years, when his shoulder wasn't fit for him to make the throws required of a third baseman. He needed to transition, mentally and physically, to playing first base, to begin anew the quest each of eight hundred or so players on each of baseball's thirty teams had every spring, to win a World Series.

"I'm excited to finally be healthy and play 155 games and

prove to everyone that I can do what I used to do," he said before that chiropractor visit. "It's almost like I have to re-prove myself. It's kind of fun—a new position, people doubting whether I can play all those games and stay healthy. It's like a second chapter."

Those are the kinds of thoughts that can help players, driving aimlessly around near their homes in the offseason with baseball on the brain. Such freeing thoughts can allow them to embrace what's to come, the seven weeks of spring training and the six months of the season to follow, a leap into what is both next-of-kin familiar and impossible to know. It is a process for every member of an organization, every player and coach and wife and scout and secretary and media relations representative. Here it comes again. Embrace it.

By January, Zimmerman was back to working out in his just-about-completed home gym. Chelsey Desmond was preparing for her first spring training staying home in Sarasota, Florida, because her third son, Ashton, had been born in October and her oldest, Grayson, had started preschool and she needed some stability. Kris Kline was back behind a screen, watching games attended by more scouts than fans, breaking in some new Nationals hires while catching up with the old ones and continuing the drive to another draft, still six months away. Doug Fister and Drew Storen had both gotten married. Tyler Moore had been to both the Dominican Republic to play winter ball and on his honeymoon to St. Lucia, a trip delayed nearly a year because when a baseball player gets married in January, spring training is too close to take time off. Rob McDonald and Mike Wallace had the upcoming season set up—flights booked, hotels reserved, equipment trucks due to arrive in February and head south down Interstate 95 to Viera, Florida, to a new season.

And right then, Mike Rizzo was working, too. The 2015 season had become "this season" for him quicker than for anyone else, out of both necessity and personality. To the outside, the Nationals' offseason had been relatively quiet—a trade of lefty Ross Detwiler for a couple of prospects, a deal that sent stalwart reliever Tyler Clippard to Oakland and brought back Yunel Escobar, a shortstop by trade whom the Nationals intended to make into their regular second base-man. Rizzo had spent most of his Christmas week at home in Chicago floored by the flu, had recovered in time to attend hockey's Winter Classic—the annual New Year's Day out-door game, staged in 2015 at Nationals Park between the hometown Capitals and Rizzo's own Chicago Blackhawks. Through it all, he rarely put down his iPhone, never over-looked a text or a call that brought an opportunity for change, for improvement. Yet at that hockey game, with a new year dawning and spring training seven weeks away, nothing seemed imminent.

But here came Scott Boras, the most prominent agent in baseball, carrying with him the prize of the offseason, right-handed pitcher Max Scherzer. In the cold of January, the quiet winter was ending.

. . .

October 10 was going to be the perfect day. Chelsey Desmond had headed back to Sarasota, leaving Ian behind in their rented home in Arlington, Virginia, for the final two weeks of the season. She was thirty-six weeks pregnant, but sometimes it was hard to tell what was more important, the coming baby or the coming playoffs. She watched on television as the Nationals clinched the division championship in Atlanta. There was little joy. "It was brutal," she said. "I hated not being there. I was just being selfish." So when the Nationals moved on to Miami for the following series, she packed up Grayson and Cruz and her pregnant self and drove south down the Gulf Coast, east across Alligator Alley, more than 225 miles to meet her husband there for some semblance of a celebration.

And in the midst of all that, they planned the way only baseball families plan. October 10 would be an off day between the first round of the playoffs and the first game of the National League Championship Series, which the Nationals would host should they advance. So a solution: If the Nationals were still playing, Ian would fly down to Sarasota the night before, the baby would be induced on that Friday the tenth, the father would be there to welcome his third son into the world and to kiss his wife, and then he'd fly back to Washington in time for a good night's rest and to play in Game 1 the following day.

So Chelsey prepared for the moment by gathering her family at the simple home in Sarasota she and Ian bought before he had earned millions of dollars, before his place in the majors was secure, and they watched the postseason play out. Even in January, the disappointment of not being in the stands still felt fresh.

"It was horrible," she said. "I hated every second of it." She and Ian would talk each day by phone. He would say, "It's fine," and she would agree, and bite her lip.

"Chelsey does a really good job of—I'm not saying *hiding* the emotions, but containing them," Ian said. "She made it pretty easy on me. I wasn't too worried about it because she didn't seem too worried about it."

She was worried about it.

"It's hard for me not to be there for him," she said. "I'm there all season, and the reason I'm there all season is to support him, and the goal the whole time is to get to the playoffs. To be there through the whole thing and they get there and I'm not there, I feel like, gosh, I should have stayed in D.C. I knew the right choice was to come home where I had help. But it was still really hard."

Kris Kline knew about the difficulty of being apart from the team he helped build. He had spent that September scouting the Giants with no way of knowing whether the Nationals would actually cross their path. But he bore down on them at a time when San Francisco was, as Kline said, "kind of limping into it." He and Doug Harris, the Nationals' director of player development, attended weeks' worth of Giants games, trying to decipher how to pitch to each player in the lineup, who was hot and should be avoided, who was slumping and should be attacked, what pitchers' tendencies were.

After the Giants beat the Pittsburgh Pirates in the wild-card game, Kline and Harris had a meeting with Nationals manager Matt Williams and the coaching staff in Washington, going over patterns of behavior, strategies, what to expect. But then he was off again, off to scout Baltimore and Detroit, American League teams the Nationals wouldn't face until the World Series. When the Nationals played, he would frequently be in another ballpark, following his employer on his phone, or watching in a hotel room, isolated.

So the tension when the Nationals lost the first game to the Giants was felt not just in Washington, not just at Nationals Park, but spread to Sarasota and Baltimore and across the country to the people who are connected to all those players in Nationals uniforms. When the Nationals held a 1–0 lead over the Giants in the second game, and Jordan Zimmermann issued a two-out walk in the ninth, and Williams came to the mound, and the bullpen door swung open for Drew Storen to jog through, hearts started beating faster hundreds of miles away. A Nationals win appeared to be minutes away. "I was pumped," Storen said.

What happened next would seem to be the kind of thing that would need a full offseason to process. Storen threw a fastball to Giants catcher Buster Posey, one of the game's best players, and Posey ripped it up the middle to put runners at first and second. For two years, Storen had worked to get back into this position, to put behind the loss to St. Louis in which he couldn't hold a lead and the season ended. He had worked to get comfortable again in the only role he had ever pursued.

"It's not like the pitch to Buster was right over the middle of the plate," Storen said. "I was ready. I felt ready. I felt like the game was slower this time."

The next hitter was Pablo Sandoval, a savvy postseason veteran who once hit three home runs in a World Series game. Storen started him with a slider for a strike, then came with another slider, down and away. Somehow, Sandoval, batting left-handed, cued the ball down the left-field line, tying the game. The Nationals would lose in eighteen innings.

"It was extremely disappointing," Storen said. "But there's no way of knowing what was going to happen. It's the ongoing debate, right? You'll never really know what would have happened if you had done something differently. It's the 'woulda coulda shoulda.' But for me, I was pitching to the style that I had thrown all year. I made the right pitch. It felt different than in '12."

So it was left to Fister to save the Nationals' season. He had watched the entire eighteen-inning affair from the dugout, watched the Giants hitters' approach to Zimmermann.

As quirky as Fister's in-between-starts approach could seem during the regular season—throwing from all angles during drills, sleeping in the hours before the first pitch—he could afford to change nothing in what could be his final appearance of the year. Down by two games, the Nationals needed to win the third to stay alive.

"You can't all of a sudden change your plan or your routine or anything else," Fister said. "I try and go about my day the same as I have for the last six months, whatever it is."

The approach had to be the same in October as it was in April. Unless you couldn't play. On August 31, Tyler Moore hit two doubles for Syracuse in a victory over Buffalo. The next day, he was across the country in Los Angeles, back in a major league uniform, back with the Nationals, where he hadn't been since late May. By that point, he had spent more time in the minors than he had wanted to—84 games with Syracuse, in which he performed adequately, hitting .265 with 10 homers. He got few chances when he was back with the big league club, with his starts coming after the Nationals had clinched the division. And when the playoffs began, the team asked him to stick around as injury insurance. So here came an odd netherworld: Not on the postseason roster, he could sit in the dugout in uniform—with no chance he could play in a game. This is what his whole season amounted to: grind in front of crowds large and small in games important and not, all so he could gaze from the dugout, with no opportunity to impact anything.

"It was tough to sit back and watch," Moore said. "It's not about you; it's about the team. You want to always show a good attitude toward that. There's a bigger picture. But it still stings a little bit."

Fister was able to delay the collective sting by pitching seven shutout innings in the third game against San Francisco, but the Nationals could push it no further. The fourth game was a blur. Moore saw everything without removing his warm-up jacket. He saw Zimmerman relegated to a pinch-hit appearance in which he popped out, Storen linger in the bullpen never to be used, Desmond go 1 for 4, and rookie reliever Aaron Barrett—Moore's Syracuse teammate for a time that summer—uncork the wild pitch that decided it in the seventh, allowing the winning run to score in a 3–2 Giants victory.

There is no overstating the car-into-a-telephone-pole suddenness of the end, particularly of something that lasted so long. It is jarring. The season, one that began when pitchers and catchers held their first workout February 15, ended 235 days later on October 7, three days before Chelsey Desmond wanted to give birth to that third son. In the loss, there was much misery, not least because another chance at all this seemed so far off, a flight home and a winter of discontent and a while to be fidgety before it all started again. But there were, too, small victories.

The Desmonds' plans to have Chelsey induced on October 10 had been thwarted because Chelsey's doctors demanded she be 39 weeks pregnant before they helped her have the baby. Chelsey's 39-week mark: October 11. "We tried," she said, "but they would not budge."

As it turned out, it didn't matter. The Desmonds' season, and all that it entails, came to a sudden stop. Their life didn't. Ian flew with the team on that red-eye, United 1809, from San Francisco to Dulles, took the bus to Nationals Park, got in his car to drive to Arlington, then flew home to Sarasota the next day, all the while in a fog of baseball and life and disappointment and impending joy.

"Obviously, we all want to win the World Series," Ian said. "But, look, sometimes you lose. And we lost. Now it's time for me to go home and be a dad. I'm not trying to make it sound like I wasn't upset. I was. It took me a long time to get over it. But I tried as hard as I could. And I have other responsibilities."

On October 11, an 8-pound, 21-inch baby boy burst forth. The season slipped away. Ashton William Desmond arrived. And that night, the National League Championship Series began—the Giants against the St. Louis Cardinals.

When 2015 dawned, Mike Rizzo was both comfortable with his team and on the lookout to change it. If the rhythm of a season is unfamiliar to even an avid fan—the early afternoons at the ballpark for a seven p.m. start, the charter flights that land at three a.m. with a game the next day—then the flow of an offseason can be even more myste-rious. Rizzo grappled with these issues every day after the season ended: Desmond, Zimmermann, Fister, center fielder Denard Span, and reliever Tyler Clippard would all be free agents following 2015. Both Desmond and Zimmermann had turned down contract extensions the previous spring. Rizzo had not reengaged them in serious negotiations. But he also couldn't find a trading partner who would yield what he thought they were worth.

What to do? The players couldn't control any of it, nor could their families. "Obviously, I see it and I hear it, but I don't pay any attention to it until someone tells me we're going somewhere else," Chelsey Desmond said. "There's no point. You'll drive yourself crazy."

So they plowed through winter. Fister got married early in November back home in California. Drew Storen got mar-ried the weekend before Thanksgiving in Indianapolis, a week after Washington infielder Danny Espinosa got mar-ried on an Arizona dude ranch. Rizzo's mind raced. His play-ers' lives went on, removed from baseball yet preparing for it still. When Storen and his bride honeymooned in Bora Bora—coincidentally where Fister and his wife took their honeymoon as well—fellow travelers noticed their Nationals-branded luggage. One of them had played with Clippard in high school. Another was a family friend of teammate Tan-ner Roark. Baseball followed him across the globe.

And in an odd way, Moore had more important work to

do than did any of them. For years, he had resisted playing winter ball in the Dominican Republic. He's a Mississippi boy, and he preferred to stay home in Mississippi. "I was stubborn about it," he said. But his twenty-eighth birthday awaited in January. The Nationals could not send him to the minors in 2015 without exposing him to other teams, so his fate with the only organization he had ever known would be determined: He would either make the major league team, or, if he didn't, he would almost certainly move on. Moore needed to try what he could, so he left behind his wife and his Brittany spaniel in Mississippi and signed up to play for Toros del Este, a Dominican team based in the eastern city of La Romana. There, on a nightly basis, he faced hard-throwing right-handed pitching, the kind he needed to be able to handle if he was to succeed in the majors.

"An experience in itself," he said. "I needed to get better, and I know I got better baseball-wise."

Through all this, Rizzo is essentially in control of their lives. Not the wedding bands and the cake choices and the guest lists, but the who-what-where-when of their professional existence. Zimmerman knew he would be back with the Nationals because he signed a $100 million extension before the 2012 season that included a no-trade clause. But beyond that, who knows?

"If this chapter closes, there's not any regret," Ian Desmond said. "That's where the peace comes from. I know the Nationals, whether they trade me or not, appreciate what I've done, and I appreciate them. I've said it a million times: I want to stay, but they have to want me to stay."

Yet part of this process of fitting into a team, of being around people more than you're around your family, is being able to exist in something of an isolation chamber. It's being ready to show up and perform regardless of who's around, no matter who leaves and who stays. There is no team sport that relies on such a fundamental individual element: batter versus pitcher. So the grind of baseball almost forces players to obsess about their own situations, with the team as a backdrop.

By the middle of January, Clippard—Storen's best friend in the game, not to mention one of the best relievers in baseball—had been traded to Oakland, a business decision. And all the while, Boras was laying the groundwork to alter the National League pennant race. Rizzo was in charge of constructing Washington's roster, but Boras had long described the pursuit of Scherzer, who won a Cy Young Award with Detroit two years earlier, as "an ownership decision." Boras met repeatedly with Theodore Lerner, the Nationals' eighty-nine-year-old managing principal owner.

In January, Boras pitched Scherzer as the Nationals' best opportunity both to win now and to serve as a stabilizing force in the future. Lerner came to Rizzo to inquire about Scherzer's baseball ability. What would he add? What are his strengths? Rizzo knew the answers intimately. In 2006, when he was still the scouting director in Arizona, Rizzo selected Scherzer, a junior at Missouri, with the eleventh pick of the draft. Rizzo loathed giving a pitcher a contract beyond six years; the history of such deals was fraught. But his input here was baseball. On January 16, Rizzo and his staff completed a slew of contracts for 2015 with current Nationals, players who were eligible for arbitration. The negotiations were fast-paced and exhausting, and Rizzo was ready to crash over the weekend. But he got a message late that day: Board meeting on Saturday morning. Dutifully, he drove to the Lerner Enterprises offices in suburban Rockville. There were the men involved in any major Nationals decision: Ted Lerner, his son Mark, his sons-in-laws Ed Cohen and Bob Tanenbaum, and Alan Gottlieb, the COO of Lerner Sports. And Rizzo faced the question: "What if we could sign Scherzer?"

Rizzo had one immediate thought: This was his team, and he didn't want to tear down one part just because another piece arrived. So he told his bosses: If this means we have to trade Zimmermann or Desmond or someone else, then I'm not on board. Ted Lerner answered: You don't have to do anything. We're going for it.

So on January 18, in the hours before the Washington wedding of one of Ted Lerner's grandsons—with Rizzo in the synagogue and at the reception—the Nationals agreed to a seven-year, $210 million contract with Max Scherzer.

Rizzo called Rob McDonald that day. "We signed Scherzer," he said. McDonald had to arrange for Scherzer to travel to Washington for his physical, had to arrange for an airport pickup, had to coordinate the doctors' visits and the hotel stays. But he was so surprised, he thought Rizzo said "Schierholtz," as in Nate, a first baseman and outfielder who had been with the Nats for a time the previous season, a bit player who might serve as spring training competition. Why, McDonald wondered, would I get this kind of call on a Sunday?

Then he realized the name in question, and it sunk in.

"We're going for it, huh?" Zimmerman said that day. Even Rizzo was stunned. He told Lerner, the only owner to whom he had ever reported directly, that he would not do the deal if it meant he had to trade Jordan Zimmermann or Desmond or Fister. The reply was direct: We're trying to win.

That night, the NFL's conference championship games were raging on, but baseball's spigot wouldn't turn off. The news leaked out in the evening, and it had ripples in Washington and Indianapolis, in the suburbs of Northern Virginia and in Sarasota. By the time Scherzer was introduced in a press conference at Nationals Park later in the week, Mike Wallace had ordered up his jersey, stitched with number 31. Storen had been through months of massage, of "evening everything out and getting back to normal," as he said, and had begun throwing. Fister had been to Bora Bora and back, and was hurling off a mound. Zimmerman was a regular at the chiropractor, part of an overhaul of his workout regimen owing to both age and experience following his hamstring problems. Desmond had grown bored of his golf clubs and paddleboard and found himself wandering around the house subconsciously wearing his baseball glove.

"Your body and your mind tells you it's time," Desmond said. "I start to see baseballs rolling around my house. I'm ready."

This business, with all the zeroes—and "Monopoly money, sometimes," Rizzo said—is part of how all these people make sense of the lives they lead. Major League Baseball is a $9 billion industry that churns forward, always generating more revenue. The players Kline identifies, the players Rizzo assembles, the players McDonald and Wallace tend to once they get to the majors—they understand it as well as anyone. Scherzer's contract might well mean there was no money left to re-sign Desmond or Jordan Zimmermann beyond 2015. As spring training approached, the cyclical nature of it all—playoff devastation, mental reconciliation, physical rest, building up again—felt a little different because of the business. Ryan Zimmerman, Jordan Zimmermann, and Desmond had known no other organization than Washington. The latter two could very well end up elsewhere in 2016.

"It would be nice to do something special in the last year we're all together," Zimmerman said. "After this year, the landscape can change. If a couple of guys are gone, the goal would be the same again, but the situation would be different. It's almost a lot more emotional for the fans than for us.

If it was up to me, I'd keep everyone and pay everyone and have the same team for ten years, but we understand that that's just not how it works. You can't keep everyone."

He hung up the phone. The chiropractor awaited.

At seven a.m. on February 9, a cold and gray Monday morning in the nation's capital, Mike Wallace and his staff began rolling boxes and crates on dollies from the home clubhouse at Nationals Park out into the concourse, which led directly to a loading dock. A 53-foot trailer arrived by 9:30 a.m., and a crew of ten movers plus Wallace's staff began packing the truck. Viera, Florida, sat 869 miles to the south. Pitchers and catchers reported in ten days.

Opening Day stood nearly two months away, the playoffs a half a year beyond that. What could be the emotion at this point? Excitement? Dread? "Both," Wallace said as the crates wheeled past him. The stacks of boxes looked endless, 30,000 pounds of equipment that needed to be loaded onto the truck. For spring training alone, Wallace had ordered 600 bats and 16,800 baseballs. One of Ian Desmond's paddleboards leaned against one wall of the loading dock, wrapped in plastic. Brought north the previous spring, it went unused in 2014 because the season—so much season—got in the way.

A Nationals employee walked through the door that led to the adjacent parking lot, found Wallace, looked at the scene, and said simply, "Another year," before shaking his hand. Wallace responded the only way he could: "Another year."

Wallace's winter had been spent working a more normal, nine-to-five-type job with his top assistant, Dan Wallin, and their staff. It had been spent with books, *Valley Forge* by Newt Gingrich, *Fenway 1912* to scratch his baseball itch, and *Killing Patton* by Bill O'Reilly, which he would take to spring training.

The banner marking the 2012 National League East Championship had been moved down the hall from the entrance to the clubhouse to make space for the new 2014 version, just to the left of the doors, right where the players would pass it on the way in. Those were the goals, what all this commotion was about. With a raw drizzle outside and not a player in sight, the goals seemed nebulous, fuzzy, far-off.

"We go through this every year," Wallace said. "Will everything fit on the truck? We always worry. And it always does."

Wallin would begin his drive of twelve hours—"If everything goes right, that is," he said—that night in his own car. Wallace would sleep at home, drive to the ballpark in the morning, hop onto the Metro to Ronald Reagan National Airport, and fly to Melbourne, Florida, where he'd pick up a rental for the short drive to Viera. Four other staff members would meet them there, and on Wednesday morning, they would start unpacking the truck, setting up spring, starting a new year.

By 1:30 p.m., the truck's back door had slammed shut. CNN played incessantly in Wallace's office, just off the entry to the Nationals' clubhouse, where each locker was empty save for a chair folded inside of it and leaning against the wall. What else was there to do but begin it all again? The truck pulled out onto Potomac Avenue, away from Nationals Park, away from Washington, and toward a new season. The grind started again.

Afterword for the Paperback Edition

As a cool autumn Sunday night turned into the wee hours of Monday morning, a Kansas City Royals reliever named Wade Davis fired a 95-mph fastball to his catcher, the backup Drew Butera. Wilmer Flores of the New York Mets didn't lift his bat, a called third strike. Davis threw his glove to the sky. The Royals leapt over the railing in the visitors' dugout at Citi Field, spilling onto the field. Kansas City celebrated. Queens slumped its shoulders and shuffled home. It was twelve thirty a.m. on November 2.

The 2015 baseball season was over. Precisely one week later, with the chill of New York all but forgotten, the general managers from all thirty clubs held their annual meetings in a posh hotel in Boca Raton, Florida.

The 2016 season began.

Perhaps more than any time in the sport's history, which stems back to the latter part of the nineteenth century, how much baseball is being played, over what period of time, is a front-and-center issue. For the Royals and Mets, 2015 began in Arizona and Florida on February 20 and 21, respectively, and ended in November, making December and January the only baseball-free months. For many of the thirty major league clubs, there were three-city road trips that included stops in three time zones. There were Sunday night games in New York followed by Monday night games in San Francisco. (Just ask the Giants.) There were, in the players' minds, far too many moments when their heads hit hotel pillows—the cushiest, deepest hotel pillows, of course—at five a.m., with a game the same night.

This is just a sliver of the baseball life, known to all who come into contact with it. Since *The Grind* was published in the summer of 2015, I have heard from fans, squinting at the rigors of baseball experience with a skeptical eye, knowing full well all the zeroes at the ends of the players' checks. There is plenty of room for a "Yeah, but . . ." followed by a story of what real working men and women do. Would the players trade places? Not a chance.

But what I have also discovered is that the nature of the baseball season is a real-life issue for all involved. Not a complaint, necessarily. Just a reality, one that increasingly determines the contours and logistics of lives. In the time since the book was published, my belief in the toll the schedule takes on players has only strengthened.

The end of the 2015 season—after midnight in November—brought, too, another inescapable element, one that players think about more than fans. The collective bargaining agreement between Major League Baseball and the players' union—the document that somehow takes athletes whose minimum salary for 2015 was $507,500 and makes them akin with the general labor force, whether they work on autos or iron—expires at the end of the 2016 season. And the leading figures on each side, Commissioner Rob Manfred and union boss Tony Clark, made clear that the logistics of the schedule—indeed, managing the toll of the grind—will be on the table for discussion, an issue in the next deal.

"In looking back from the time I played, now that I'm watching what these guys do, I don't know how they do it," Clark, a big-league first baseman from 1995 to 2009, said last summer. "I really don't. What the guys are being asked to do with respect to start times, with respect to the travel distances, with respect to performing at an elite level with three days off a month? It's a challenge. And I think that's why, as we move forward and guys continue to be asked to do more and more, I think we need to look at it significantly."

It is the fabric of the game. And the fabric of the game is wearing on people.

"We're at a point in time where any number of things the guys are being asked to do are directly affecting the way they play," Clark continued. "And that's not beneficial for anybody."

. . .

The 2015 season didn't go as planned for the Washington Nationals. That the Mets, rather than the Nationals, won the National League East and advanced to the World Series seemed unlikely when 2014 came to a close, when the trucks were packed for spring training in Viera, Florida, the following February.

The season, for fans, will be remembered as a disappointment, the 79 losses somehow outweighing the 83 wins. The players agreed. "I look at this as an opportunity lost," said Jayson Werth, the veteran outfielder, one of several key players who spent weeks of the year unable to play because of injury.

But the scope of that season, in which the World Series favorites failed to even make the playoffs, made the grind of careers apparent, too. The events in this book take place during the 2014 season and the offseason that followed. Yet that time frame is, essentially, arbitrary. It was always about any team in any season, the characters replicated across the game.

What happened to the Nationals in 2015 only enhances that.

Ryan Zimmerman, the veteran, spent yet another offseason trying to put the injuries of 2014 behind him—only to suffer more injuries. "Don't feel bad for me," Zimmerman said one day in the midst of it, and that is the perspective a $100 million contract gives. Still, he had to deal with the frustration of a nagging foot problem—plantar fasciitis, they called it—that left him unable to transfer his weight during his at-bats or stop properly after running. Ultimately, it left him unable to play. Back when he was twenty-two, Zimmerman played in all 162 games of the 2007 season. In 2014 and 2015 combined, he played in 156, his body defying him more frequently than ever.

Ian Desmond entered 2015 with much on his mind, his family at the forefront. He and his wife, Chelsey, welcomed their third son, Ashton, just days after the Nationals' playoff loss. That meant some adjustments for the family as 2015 dawned. Ian, too, had to adjust to the notion that the season would likely be his last in Washington. The headlines are easy to see: *Ian Desmond will be a free agent at the end of the year, and he and the Nationals aren't talking about a new contract.* The impact on the family isn't as streamlined. The couple's older sons, Grayson and Cruz, owned all manner of Nationals gear. They watched Nationals games. Their heroes were their dad's teammates, other Nationals.

On the field, with a personal and professional shift on the way, Ian Desmond struggled. There was no other way to look at it. He began the year with an error that led to the winning run on Opening Day, and in some ways it got worse from there. He hit for a lower average, reached base less frequently, and struck out more often than he ever had. Through it, Chelsey tried to prop him up. She reminded him that he was a good husband. She reminded him that he was a good father. She reminded him that he was doing right by their family.

"All the stuff that I should be thinking and, in a normal state of mind, all the stuff that I *would* be thinking," Ian said.

Within the rhythm of the baseball season, in the midst of its everydayness, there must somehow be room for major developments, for crises. By August 2015, Doug Fister, the starter, was no longer starting, banished to the bullpen after the first four months of his season were interrupted by injury and marred by substandard performance. Drew Storen, the reliever, was demoted from his job as closer because the team traded for *another* closer, veteran Jonathan Papelbon. Tyler Moore, the twenty-sixth man, wasn't toggling back-and-forth to the minor leagues, but he was struggling to hit even .200 in the majors.

To one degree or another, they all had crises midstream.

"What can I do other than try to find some sort of positive in the situation?" Fister said.

These are, in the midst of months when the team had just two days off—as the Nationals did in both August and September—career-altering changes. And they can, taken all together, alter the course of a franchise.

As the Nationals sputtered to the finish in 2015, Zimmerman was out of the lineup with an oblique injury, Desmond tried to stave off the most uncertain offseason of his career, Fister tried to adapt to a new role, and Storen allowed some of the hits that truly sank the season—a three-run double to Yoenis Cespedes of the Mets that completed a six-run

comeback for New York one night, a two-run homer to Cespedes the following night that completed a devastating three-
game sweep.

That was the last inning Storen would pitch for the Nationals. When he returned to the clubhouse after that inning, he
sat dazed in a chair in front of his locker. When the Mets
recorded the final out, he stood up and slammed shut the door
to the cubbyhole above the space that held his clothes. He
caught his thumb on a piece of metal, and broke it.

In January, he was traded to the Toronto Blue Jays.

There would be no October for the Nationals, and that
meant Mike Rizzo, the general manager, needed to evaluate
changes. On the team's last home stand, Rizzo was all but
knocked out in his condominium, floored by a debilitating
back problem. He watched on television as Papelbon, his
key trade-deadline acquisition, challenged Bryce Harper, the
team's best player who was finishing off an MVP season, for
loafing on a routine fly ball. The kicker on Rizzo's year: he
couldn't be in the clubhouse in the moments after Papelbon
choked Harper in the dugout, with television cameras catching it all.

That day, Matt Williams, the team's manager, sent Papelbon back out to the mound after the fight. "He's our closer,"
Williams said afterward. No player or coach in the dugout
had alerted Williams to the fracas.

On the day after the season ended, Rizzo fired Williams.

As the postseason played out without the Nationals, Rizzo and his bosses—members of the Lerner family, who own the team—interviewed candidates to be the new manager, the new leader, the new face. The players scattered nationwide, beginning their own decompression. Rizzo's season, with no games to be played, found another gear. After extensive interviews, the team offered the managerial job to Bud Black, who had previously managed the San Diego Padres. But Black was put off by the club's initial offer. This information leaked out to the media. It embarrassed the club and angered the Lerners.

There was no baseball being played, but this was not a good time to be Mike Rizzo. The team moved quickly to reach a deal with Dusty Baker, who had previously taken the Giants, Cubs, and Reds to the playoffs. The outcome, from the player and public perspective, was fine. But the entire process stressed out Rizzo, who hadn't even begun the process of fixing the roster.

By the time the sport's annual winter meetings convened in Nashville in early December, a left-handed pitcher named David Price had signed a seven-year, $217 million contract with the Boston Red Sox, a record for a free-agent pitcher. There is more money in the game than ever; baseball's revenues approached $9.5 billion in 2015. There is no indication that number will go down.

Yet reporting and writing this book, then watching

another season through the prism it provides, has me thinking about baseball differently than I did five or ten years ago.
Back then, I thought of the contracts and the careers and
how much each and every one of us, playing out imaginary
two-on-two-out scenarios in our backyards, would have killed
to be where these guys were, to live the lives they have. The
money is enormous, and they're playing out their dreams—
all of our dreams.

But the 2015 season, stretching from February until that
final out on an early November morning, reinforced that as
much as the game is a game, the players have a job that is just
that: a job, regardless of the glitz that goes with it, regardless
of the fun they have along the way. For us, the baseball season is a nightly reality show, flickering on the television set
from seven to ten p.m. all summer long. What we don't see
are the countless, subtle, blue-collar machinations that go
into the production. Think about them when you flip on the
games this year—the road trip your team is in the midst of
and what went into pulling it off, the stress of a potential
trade, the wife and kids back home, the scout scouring the
earth for more players, the pitcher worried about losing his
job, the fringe guy dreading the demotion to the minors, the
executive wondering whether to keep a manager or get rid of
him. They all live that life, daily. It's inescapable.

So 2015, like any other season, enhanced one of the game's
truisms for me: no season is longer, none is less relenting, than

baseball's. It was true last year. It will be true next year. Whether your job is to hit homers or pack bags, to trade players or evaluate them, to retire the first batter or the last, that wake-up-and-play-again quality defines baseball, now and forever.

Washington, D.C.
January 2016

ACKNOWLEDGMENTS

This wasn't supposed to be a book. But at the beginning of every year, a bunch of us sportswriters at *The Washington Post* come up with story lists for the next twelve months—tales we'd like to pursue and tell. That's what this book was: an entry on a proposed story list, albeit a bit more involved, because the idea was to use six pieces to show how playing baseball nearly every day can impact everyone who comes in contact with a major league team—in this case the local nine, the Washington Nationals.

So before it became a book, someone had to allow it to become a newspaper series. Matt Vita, the *Post*'s sports editor, is always ready to support an enterprising idea, and he jumped on it, as did his deputy Matt Rennie, who will always be my first editor at the paper and my good friend. Their support was essential. Tracee Hamilton, who served as my editor when the franchise first arrived in Washington from Montreal, curated the copy with her usual careful touch, treating the stories as if they were her own. The indispens-able Mitch Rubin directed the traffic to make sure all the elements looked splendid online.

In order for this to be a series in a newspaper, much less a book, I had to have willing subjects. A nod first, then, to Ryan Zimmerman, a star in Washington who has never much acted like one around me. I first met Zimmerman the day after he was drafted as a twenty-year-old out of the University of Virginia, back in June 2005. Even in the years when I wasn't regularly around the team, I could reach out to him if I needed some baseball perspective. He would always provide it. He always made time. So it was in January 2014, when I needed to start this series, that I felt comfortable starting with Zim, because I suspected he would understand the story I was trying to tell, and that he would be willing to help tell it. He did, and he was. The series, and the book, couldn't have existed if he didn't buy in from the start.

I guess, in a way, I'd known Ian Desmond even longer, because we first met at spring training 2005, when Desmond was a nineteen-year-old just a year out of high school thrust into the spotlight of a big league camp. He may have taken the most significant leap of faith here, because—early in the series, before people knew really what to make of it—he offered to talk to his wife, Chelsey, about the prospect of helping out, of telling their story as a family. And he made a bold decision: Ian said the family's participation was completely up to Chelsey. When she said yes, she unknowingly chose to represent all baseball wives. There really was nothing in it for the Desmonds other than to explain that a baseball marriage is different, that it might not be what you'd expect. I'm eternally grateful to both of them—not to mention little Grayson and Cruz—for opening up themselves and their home, because now so many more people have an understanding of what it's like.

So thanks to all the participants, each of whom gave more than I could have expected and each of whom appears here. Kris Kline allowed a reporter and photographer to wander into a ballpark in Alabama, sit in the stands with him as he scouted prospects, then ride shotgun all the way to Atlanta before boarding a flight the next morning and doing the drill all over again. I can't remember a reporting trip on which I learned more. Doug Fister took the time, over several q-and-a sessions, to explain why off days for pitchers are just workdays out of the spotlight. Tyler Moore allowed a reporter and a photographer to meet him on the road in the minors, welcoming us into the clubhouse and his home away from home. Rob McDonald went out of his way to make sure I understood every detail of what goes into a road trip, and Mike Wallace didn't mind me hanging around in his office during a game or in the hotel lobby as he packed bags. They were cooperative, accommodating subjects who by nature deflect attention, but they allowed us to pay some anyway.

Even after the series had been printed in the *Post* over the course of the summer, Drew Storen so grasped the idea behind it that he made time to talk about his place in it, and opened his home in September as the playoffs approached. And Mike Rizzo helped with so much, not only outlining his own job and style, but chatting about and encouraging his old buddy Kline and approving access to the clubhouse during a game, to a team bus ride, and onto the tarmac in Atlanta, where I could report on a road trip's machinations.

In all of this, the Nationals' public relations staff, led by John Dever and assisted by Amanda Comak and Kyle Brostowitz, constantly asked what I needed, encouraged players and staff to participate, and absolutely helped where other organizations may have hindered. I probably asked Matt Williams, the first-year manager, about some aspect of every single chapter, and he never failed to come through. Randy Knorr has so many different perspectives—player, minor league manager, major league coach—he was always worth bouncing off an idea or two. Add in Harolyn Cardozo, who just gets it, and the Nationals were the perfect franchise around which to try to pull this off. Thanks to all.

Since I arrived at the *Post* in 2003, we have been encouraged to pursue such projects. Had this series merely lived in the *Post*'s pages and on the Web site, I would have been satisfied. It was fun to report, fun to write, fun to see land on the page and the computer screen.

But a book is a different endeavor. For this to happen, someone needed to have a bold idea. That would be Rick Maese, *Post* sportswriter, partner at the paper and over lunch and over bourbon, who one day said, "You should make those stories into a book."

So thanks to Rick, because you wouldn't be reading these pages if he hadn't muttered that over lunch. Rick and fellow *Post* sportswriters Dave Sheinin (the best writer on an exceptional staff) and Adam Kilgore (the best beat writer in Nationals history) took the time to read each of the chapters that ran in the paper, offering suggestions and improvements that are, in turn, reflected in these pages. Sally Jenkins is always quick with encouragement, which—coming from the country's best sports columnist—matters. And there are times I still find myself picking up my jaw from the floor when I realize, "I'm talking baseball with Thomas Boswell in this press box." In the decade-plus I've worked with Boz—side by side on baseball, the Redskins, and golf—I've fed off his energy and learned something, about sports or writing or both, every single day. An honor and a privilege.

The paper's exceptional sports photographers also were essential in telling the story and a blast to work with— Jonathan Newton on Zimmerman and Kline, Toni Sandys on the Desmonds and Moore, John McDonnell on Fister, McDonald, and Wallace. Thanks for your patience and your pictures.

Now, to make this a book: Esther Newberg, my agent at ICM, took about five minutes to find the perfect fit for this project. That would be with David Rosenthal at Blue Rider, who believed in the original pieces and saw how they could be expanded. The *Post*, too, had to support the series again—and beyond its own walls. So thanks to managing editor Kevin Merida for navigating that world, to executive editor Marty Baron for pushing it through, and to Tracy Grant for dealing with the logistics. And, of course, to Emilio Garcia-Ruiz for hiring me in the first place.

And, then, my family, most important not only because they deal with my foibles but because they were there first. A special thanks to my mom, Kay, for dusting off her skills as an English teacher and giving the manuscript a thorough read. Towering above them all: my wife, Susan, who offered support for all of this as a newspaper series and as a book, who relished playing with our little daughter, Molly, when I had to go work on it, and who supports me every single day. She is the best.

February 2015

ABOUT THE AUTHOR

Barry Svrluga has worked at *The Washington Post* since 2003 and is currently the national baseball writer. He previously reported on and blogged about the Washington Nationals and is the author of *National Pastime*, which details the franchise's relocation from Montreal and its first season in the nation's capital. He lives in Washington, D.C., with his wife and daughter.